THE

GREATEST
INVENTION

THE GREATEST INVENTION

A HISTORY OF THE WORLD
IN NINE MYSTERIOUS SCRIPTS

SILVIA FERRARA

TRANSLATED FROM THE ITALIAN BY
TODD PORTNOWITZ

FARRAR, STRAUS AND GIROUX
New York

Farrar, Straus and Giroux
120 Broadway, New York 10271

Printed in the United States of America
Originally published in Italian in 2019 by Giangiacomo Feltrinelli Editore,
Italy, as *La grande invenzione*
English translation published in the United States by Farrar, Straus and Giroux
First American edition, 2022

Illustration credits can be found on page 291.

Library of Congress Cataloging-in-Publication Data
Names: Ferrara, Silvia, author. | Portnowitz, Todd, 1986– translator.
Title: The greatest invention : a history of the world in nine mysterious scripts /
    Silvia Ferrara ; translated from the Italian by Todd Portnowitz.
Other titles: Grande invenzione. English
Description: First American edition. | New York : Farrar, Straus and Giroux,
    2022. | Includes bibliographical references.
Identifiers: LCCN 2021044938 | ISBN 9780374601621 (hardcover)
Subjects: LCSH: Writing—History. | Inscriptions—History. | Extinct languages.
Classification: LCC P211 .F42713 2022 | DDC 411.09—dc23/eng/20211115
LC record available at https://lccn.loc.gov/2021044938

Our books may be purchased in bulk for promotional, educational, or business
use. Please contact your local bookseller or the Macmillan Corporate and
Premium Sales Department at 1-800-221-7945, extension 5442, or by email at
MacmillanSpecialMarkets@macmillan.com.

www.fsgbooks.com
www.twitter.com/fsgbooks • www.facebook.com/fsgbooks

10 9 8 7 6 5 4 3 2 1

This book is an output of the ERC project INSCRIBE (Invention of Scripts
and Their Beginnings). The project has received funding from the European
Research Council (ERC) under the European Union's Horizon 2020 research
and innovation program (Grant Agreement No. 771127).

Contents

Ante Litteram 3

BEHIND THE SCENES

Stories

Fiction 7

Spark 9

Armchair Inventors 11

Nature

The Line 14

Things 16

Icons 18

Symbols 22

UNDECIPHERED SCRIPTS

Islands

Crete

Face Forward 29

Pioneers 31

As Good as New 32

House of Cards 34

Stray Cat 36

Syllables 40

Lost Language? 42

Cyprus

Mixtures 45

1-2-3 47

Mine 50

The King's Marbles 53
Almost There? 56
Intermission 57

Easter Island

The Center of the World 60
Miracle 62
Dodo's Egg 66
Watch Your Back 69
Tantalus 72
Rebus 74

INVENTED SCRIPTS

Cities

Bureaumania 83
An Imperfect Match 86
Invention, Intention 92
The Forest 94

Before the Pharaohs

Marketing 98
The Grammar of Creation 101
Encroachment 105
The Stone Guest 108
Sliding Doors 110

Between Two Rivers

Tokenism 113
Silent Moviola 116
The Ambiguous Rebus 119
United Nations 121

Chinese Turtles

From Scratch 127
A Disaster-Free Week? 129
The Glorious Life of Lady Hao 132
Don't Call Them Ideograms 134

Across the Ocean

It Could Have Gone Worse *138*

False Start, Long Life *142*

Emojis *147*

Living Souls *150*

End of Story

Commonalities *153*

Diderot *156*

EXPERIMENTS

Tradition

Telephone *161*

Flops *162*

Solitary Inventors

Blues Brothers *166*

Migraine *168*

The Alchemist *170*

The Asemic *175*

The Wizard *176*

The Illiterate *179*

Isolated Branches

Pokémon *182*

Inca Paradox *183*

Talking Knots *186*

Beta Software *187*

Darkness *189*

Chutes and Ladders *192*

Black Swan *195*

Bestiary of the Indus *196*

Entropy *200*

Social Inventors

Reaching an Agreement *204*

Brad Pitt *206*

Alignments *210*
Scrabble, Chess, and Scripts *212*
Better to Be in Bad Company *214*

DISCOVERIES
Where to Begin
Quartet *219*
Donald Rumsfeld *221*
Any Other Stone *225*
Scratch and Win *228*
The Gold *232*
Ten Commandments *234*

How to Decipher
Extraction *237*
Five Easy Pieces *239*
And Now for the Sixth *243*
Ex Machina *246*

THE GREAT VISION
First
Evolution *255*
Necessity *257*
Memory *260*

Afterward
Late to the Party *265*
Out of Sync *267*
Mailbox *268*
After the Wheel *270*

Tomorrow
Icons: The Sequel *272*
Dead Letter *274*

Postscriptum *279*

Essential Bibliography *285*

THE

GREATEST

INVENTION

Ante Litteram

I'm in fifth grade and my teacher makes a few strange marks on the chalkboard, signs I've never seen before. It's spring 1986 and, at ten years old, I can barely read. I'm a little behind for my age: learning to write was a long and laborious undertaking.

But in that moment my teacher writes something on the board—and without knowing it, she inscribes my future. She was dressed in white, I remember, like the chalk marks on the blackboard. *Alpha beta gamma.* I tried to decode them. There are only so many moments like this in a life, moments in which some gesture vacuums up the space around you and carries it off into time. The years pass, and your memory warps and skews and often flattens the details—but those few scrawlings slashed like the blade of a knife. Thirty years later, I can still hear the chalk's staccato sizzle. The Greek alphabet tattooed itself onto my skin. I could never have known that I'd spend my life trying to make sense of the world's illegible signs, why they look the way they do, what they might possibly mean. I could never have known that I'd forge a life from trying to decipher.

This is not a book on Ancient Greek, or on the alphabet. Nor is it a history lesson. This book is *almost* a story about invention, the greatest invention in the world. And I say *almost* because it has a beginning, and it carries us on a journey around the world, filled with adventure, but the end remains to be written.

The greatest invention in the world. Without it, we would be only voice, suspended in a continual present. The most solid and profound part of our being is forged in memory, in the desire to anchor ourselves to something stable, to persist, knowing well that our time is limited. This book speaks of that urgent need to remain, of the bond we share with others, the dialogue we hold with ourselves. This book recounts the invention of writing.

The protagonists of our tale, however, are not the scripts alone, nor those who discovered or deciphered them. We ourselves are the protagonists—our brains, our ability to communicate and interact with the life that surrounds us. Writing is an entire world to be discovered, but it is also a filter through which to observe our own, *our* world: language, art, biology, geometry, psychology, intuition, logic. It has things to say about who we are, as human beings capable of feeling, of experiencing and inspiring emotions. This book recounts an uncharted journey, one filled with past flashes of brilliance, present-day scientific research, and the faint, fleeting echo of writing's future.

BEHIND THE
SCENES

Stories

FICTION

We human beings love to invent stories. Baboons, though no less fascinating than us, spend only 10 percent of their time interpreting, adopting, and imitating others' actions. The rest of their time they dedicate to finding food and nourishment. Our percentages are the complete opposite.

We spend an astonishing amount of time trying to understand others—putting ourselves in their shoes, empathizing, acting as a mirror for their emotions and intentions. This tendency has been a major force in the development of our social intelligence. Other factors, of course, have played a role, but we are the only species that uses imagination. Every day we create real, probable, possible, impossible, and absurd scenarios. An infinity of fictions, one layered atop the other.

We create things that don't exist in nature, such as symbols. Along with histories, laws, institutions, governments. All of this is made up. And all of it hinges on the exchange of information: storytelling, forging alliances, establishing and disrupting social equilibriums, gossip.

And yet there's an order to it. Studies of modern hunter-gatherers in the Kalahari Desert or in the Philippines reveal stark differences in the ways they communicate. In the day-time, their discussions revolve around practical matters, lo-cation, food—along with a certain amount of chatter about one's position within the group, climbing the social ladder, competition. Highly personal and logistical matters, noth-ing fanciful. When they gather in the evening, however, after the hunt, their interactions grow more relaxed. They lower their guard. Seated around the fire, under the light of the moon, they tell stories, they sing, they dance. Their bond grows tighter and stronger.

That's how it always goes: when we relax, it's as if we give voice to our imagination. Don't the best ideas come the moment you stop racking your brain? Think about when you're standing around the office kitchen with your colleagues, or when you call your wife/husband to discuss what/where to eat for dinner, or when you trash-talk your boss. Now think about your evenings, when you coax your children to sleep with a fairy tale, or glue yourself to Net-flix, or let it all go at the club or a concert. Think about how, deep down, over the course of hundreds of thousands of years, our communication, and all the structures we've developed to facilitate it, has hardly changed at all.

To prove it, I'm going to tell you two overarching sto-ries. Two stories that are very different from each other—each, in turn, containing many smaller stories within it, threads that never intersect. These smaller threads are very similar, they share many ingredients, even if they're not connected, but the overarching stories are decidedly different. One is filled with detectives, pursuit, aspiration, reward; the other with calmness, time, growth, patience, control. One speaks of unresolved enigmas, the other of inventions. One speaks of attempts and sudden disappear-ances, the other of plots with happy endings. You'll have little trouble figuring out which is which. At the end of the day, in any case, they're only stories.

SPARK

Before we wade deeper into these stories, however, we'll need to address a few preliminary questions. First of all, it will help to have at least a provisional answer to the question "How is a script born?" For this, we'll need to jump back to the *beginning* beginning, the start of it all. Back, that is, to the moment when symbols were born, when the depiction of a thing became the specific name for that thing. I draw a horse and, if I'm able to articulate language (as was *Homo sapiens*, and perhaps even the Neanderthals, thousands of years ago), I call it "horse." Prehistoric art is exquisite, fascinating, highly refined even, but it is enigmatic: the drawing of a horse may very well mean something else. Perhaps it isn't your basic Paleolithic nag, but some creature of the imagination: a hornless unicorn, a wingless Pegasus. Whatever it truly is, we'll never know. The same enigma that lures us in very happily boots us out.

And even then, a drawing is just a drawing—it's charged with potential, but ultimately wordless. It remains mute. As have millions of drawings, over thousands of years, in hundreds of different places around the world. The Sumerians, too, five thousand years ago in Mesopotamia, drew objects and numbers on clay tablets.

On these tablets, they recorded small economic transactions related to the Mesopotamian temples. Think of it like a grocery list, where the symbols are placed in a scattered (dis)order. A kind of protohistoric stenography, with (nonphonetic) symbols linked to numbers.

If I were to ask you if this is writing, you'd say no. And I'd agree. But here the stage is being set for a daring, dazzling intuition that will render its invention possible. And not only in Mesopotamia, 3,100 years before the birth of Christ, but in China, Egypt, and Central America, too—in different periods, but always in the same way, following the same brilliant flash of intuition. Four magical moments, separate and independent, where a spark was lit and the wheels of invention began to turn. And for all we know, in the history of our world, there may well have been other such inventions.

And if you think it's tough to reimagine that moment, buried as it is beneath centuries and centuries, beneath layers and layers of reconstruction, you're wrong. What's amazing is that we can nearly capture the scene, as in a film: our little Mesopotamian fellow, working his clay, taking his stylus in hand. We can see him sitting there on his stool, forging a tablet. The tablet is small and he carves little boxes, to group the objects he wants to count. He counts them. Marks down their number. They're things that must be reimbursed to the temple. In the upper right-hand corner he draws a cane (as in a reed): cane, in Sumerian, is *gi*, but *gi* can also mean something else, the verb "to reimburse."

Magic. Or better yet, surprise. The sound is the same, but the meaning is completely different. All at once he realizes that he can use the symbol of a cane to say something else, something he clearly doesn't know how to write. And this is what he does—he takes the logogram and changes its meaning, without altering the sound at all. Unintentionally, almost instinctually, his Sumerian neurons start to fire. He has made—he has *recorded*—a play on words. We call this principle homophony, and it's very simple, intuitive, natural. As we'll see, we still use it today—it comes to us spontaneously, and sometimes it even makes us laugh. Brushing away the dust of centuries past, I can imagine our Mesopotamian man, writing away and smiling at his sudden discovery. It's the same face I make when I get a text with a homophonic emoji. Now, whether or not this man knew what he was getting himself into is another matter—and it's highly unlikely he did.

ARMCHAIR INVENTORS

We must be careful when we talk about the invention of writing. Inventing writing is not a mechanical process. It's not a matter of precisely and intentionally choosing signs to represent sounds, to create a perfectly functional and efficient system.

Nor should we be picturing the priestly and ethereal scribe, alone and intent, bent over his work on a rainy or muggy afternoon, drawing little squiggles that give shape to proto-cuneiform or Old Chinese in the matter of a day.

Which is not to say that there aren't cases where a script was invented ad hoc by a lone individual. We'll encounter a few in this book—like the script invented by Sequoyah, who in 1821 took the Latin and Greek alphabets by the scruff and wrangled them into a writing system for the Cherokee language. The achievement would make him a national hero. Or else the alphabet invented by Hildegard of Bingen, a twelfth-century Benedictine abbess. Or there's the Cameroonian king Njoya, who toward the end of the nineteenth century created a semi-syllabary for the Bamum people. But these creations are derivative, artificial, and, particularly in the case of the Bamum, imposed from on high, by those who govern.

Writing wasn't invented in an armchair.

The invention of writing—especially when we mean writing invented from nothing, from scratch—came about as a process, a series of coordinated, cumulative, and gradual actions.

Writing as a complete *system*, structured and organized, was the work of many. By communicating, exchanging opinions, arguing it out, and eventually coming to an agreement, this multitude built a common, approved, standardized repertoire of signs.

Writing is therefore a *social* invention, where alignment, coordination, and feedback play essential roles. All of which we'll see ample evidence of in the chapters to come.

In the same regard, writing was not invented in the blink of an eye, but in stages. It is a machine with thousands of gears, and in many cases it took several generations to develop. As we'll see, the road to writing's invention was filled with experiments, attempts, adjustments. It is therefore also a *gradual* process, a process of reiteration and transmission.

Now let's look at the letters, the ones you're reading on this page, or those from any other system—Arabic, Hebrew, Georgian, Chinese. Look at how the signs are drawn. What makes them the shape they are and not some other shape; why are there *this* many signs and not more; who determined which sounds to write down and which to leave out? These are the ingredients of true invention. The long process of negotiation, the shared effort, the building of an ordered and complete system. Finished, polished.

All of which leads us to see writing as a cultural product, not something inherent. As a kind of technology, an object, an artifact. And yet its shapes are the shapes we find in the world around us, and in all its contours. They follow the anatomy of our visual perception; they adapt to the things that surround us and that capture our attention. And the sounds behind these signs lend themselves to spontaneous wordplay; they engage our innate capacity to manipulate meanings, to lose ourselves in abstraction, to create far-fetched associations, to see symbols. Writing is a thing we've created, yes, but it is also deeply ingrained in our versatile ability to see with our own eyes while—at the same time, in the same moment, and almost by magic—seeing the world through the very different eyes of others. It's all right there, crammed into our endlessly surprising human nature, even when we're busy creating such a stubborn and static material object.

Nature

Take a look at the objects around you. Look at how they're positioned, their lines and outlines: How do they intersect? What shapes do they make? The window jambs form rectangles. Tabletops form Ls where they meet the legs. There's the T between double doors, the D of an armchair's oval backrest. The vertical lines of utility poles, the upside-down Vs of mountains, the circles of the sun, asterisks of the stars, skein of tangled twine, curling and coiling computer wires.

There's an alphabet in things, and it's no coincidence. If you pay attention, if you really look, you'll see that all around you is an architecture of letters, emerging from the shapes of things. It seems almost obvious: our sense of vision is much more alert to lines, to contrasts, than to the flat or formless surfaces that contain them. What's happening at the edges, the borders, the interstices—that's what strikes our eyes. What's between is of much less interest. The scientists who discovered this, Hubel and Wiesel, did so almost by accident, and it won them a Nobel Prize.

We are fundamentally visual creatures—animals that, like few others, rely on our vision to orient ourselves in the world. Among our senses, sight is dominant. Yet we've only recently discovered how vision and the visual cortex function. In the 1950s, the neurophysiologist David Hubel began recording the activity of visual cells, using cats as his guinea pigs. The experiments dragged on for years (as you can imagine, given what we know about herding cats).

Hubel's approach was to record the cats' brain activity while black and white blobs were projected on a screen. How did they perceive them? Trial after trial, the blobs produced no effect. Their amorphous shapes triggered no neuronal activity. No spike on the cat encephalogram. Until, one day, while running a glass slide with a blob painted on it through the projector, they noticed that the edge of the slide made a line on the screen. And finally, something sparked in their feline brains: a line, no matter how faint, caught the retina's attention. The line's irresistible allure.

The edges and contours of our surrounding environment are the first step to absorbing and understanding the world around us. Our brain feeds us images in pixels, the tesserae of a mosaic that we must reconstruct. It does not project, like a movie screen, all that's happening before our eyes. And the most elementary pixels, the world's first tesserae, are contours. Not what lies between them.

And if edges are indeed what capture our neurons' attention, it makes perfect sense that, hiding in the lines and configurations of the things around us, we find an alphabet much like the one we know. In fact, the frequencies are constant. If we look at the signs in every writing system throughout history, with no regard for when or where they were created or used, we find that the frequency of their shapes remains the same. Line-segment combinations like the ones that form an L or a T have the same distribution frequency (high) across writing systems (even those from very distant historical periods). X and F are less frequent.

What's surprising is that the same distribution regularity we find across writing systems also applies to shapes in the natural world.

It's as if writing, in its evolution, sought to copy nature's contours, to make itself easier to perceive and simpler to read. Just like the line that captured the attention of Hubel's cats. The neurons in our brain, whether by intuition or by a natural predisposition, selected shapes that resembled things we'd already seen before and were therefore recognizable. Which is to say that our process for perceiving objects was recycled, almost boorishly, for another purpose: to recognize written signs. And I say *boorishly* because the invention of writing stole space for itself in our brain—even if, physiologically, nothing changed. The stolen space was already there (the occipital-temporal area), though it was tasked with another function: the visual perception of objects. Neuron recycling at its best. Through a process of subtracting, toying with shapes, and above all simplifying, human beings not only created something that wasn't there before, but, over time, and almost naturally, rendered it easy to recognize. Not always so easy to perceive, as we'll see, much less to decipher. But there you have it: nature's alphabet, woven into writing's DNA.

Nulla dies sine linea, as Pliny the Elder said. No day without a line. Now lift your head, and start looking for the letters all around you.

THINGS

This discourse on the line is valid for "linear" scripts (obviously)—those that are stylistically advanced and that don't resemble other immediately recognizable things, like a hand, or a foot, or a tree. Such signs carry clear reference points, which complicates things a bit, since we recognize depictions only because we've previously seen the thing being depicted—though levels of familiarity can vary widely, and are often subjective. Writing is born of a desire to name the things we see, to fix them in place. Not verbs or actions, but lists of things.

We could here delve into a long and heady discussion on the concept of "things," but best to leave that to the philosophers. One Greek fable recounts the story of Thales, who, lost in thought as he studied the sky, walked himself right into a well. A young girl passing by teased him: "You want to know the things of the universe, but what about the things right in front of your eyes?" Ancient Greek uses *ta* for everything, a single syllable with a barrelful of meanings. But the contrast here is with concrete things, such as holes in the middle of the street.

Let us start, then, from concreteness. The bond between writing and "things" has always been a strong one. Both are, by definition, firm and lasting entities. Let's try an experiment: grab a pen and paper and *draw one thing*. I'll give you thirty seconds. What did you draw? An object, in all likelihood. A house? A bike? A Hershey's kiss? We'd arrive at the same result, though perhaps with less predictability, if I asked you to *think of one thing*. You wouldn't think of happiness or relativity or destiny—you'd think of something concrete.

All writing is founded on this concreteness. And it's no different today. Think about what we do when we want to indicate actions, which are abstract concepts and therefore more difficult to represent. Take, for example, the recycling bin on your computer screen, which in one concise image suggests the act of "throwing away," "deleting." Or the magnifying lens: "to search." And (nearly all) emojis: an airplane does not mean "to airplane" but "to fly," a heart is not "to heart" but "to love," a thumbs-up says, "I like this." The action is expressed by the instrument used to evoke it or that renders it possible.

Things persist in time. They're not fleeting like movements or gestures or actions. When we communicate them, especially when we draw or write them, we express a profound intuition: we embrace the cognitive persistence of objects, which brings them into greater focus, makes them more immediate. More solid. This is where they are and this is where they'll stay. Actions have a dynamic element that's harder to carry over to the page: actions are made of movement, gestures dissolve in air.

Writing is just the opposite: material, fixed in place, immobile. It's static, like things.

Even actions, once written down, grind to a halt. They're reified—they become "things." With the result that writing's strength, its permanence, is also its greatest limit: writing, like things, *stays put.*

ICONS

The lists of things with which writing first comes into being are composed of familiar icons. A bowl, an ear of wheat, a horse, a mountain, a fish.

These early icons are creative, drawn with variety but also with precision. Their relationship with reality is based upon resemblance and analogy, and therefore comes in degrees: the part for the whole (the head of an ox for the whole animal, the delta of the pubis for a woman); a bare-bones outline to represent something more complex (waves for

water, a star for the heavens). But there's one unifying factor: the drawings must be recognizable. This is true for all
icons. Whether painted or drawn, an icon's form and meaning must be in clear dialogue with each other, leaving no
chance for arbitrary interpretation: one simply "reads" them
on the spot. Familiarity can come in a million flavors—as
long as the icon-image bears the imprint of an object with a
precise name, that's all that matters.

We've been grilling ourselves about this for centuries,
testing the link between the names we give to things and
their reality. Is it that we simply call up a name and slap
it to whatever object, entity, thing? Or do names naturally
capture the essence of what they represent, without artifice?

It's a sticky subject, names and their relation to the
objects they represent. What if our names are all naked,
substance-free? Plato: names mislead, and it's not always
resemblance that determines them, but habit. Shakespeare,
there's no relation at all: *a rose by any other name would
smell as sweet*—Romeo and Juliet's love would be just as
true even if his last name were Johnson. Convention, habit,
tradition. And then, a century ago, came the coup de grâce,
from the father of modern linguistics himself, Saussure: no
natural resemblance exists between names and things; signifier and signified are detached, only weakly, whimsically,
arbitrarily related. And that's how the rose, and everything
else, got its name. End of story.

These days, in truth, we're not so militant in our belief.
Yes, the connection between words and nature is fickle, but
sometimes it can feel remarkably on target. Iconicity, when
it occurs, can truly make us see, and even feel. Sign language, for example, is visual iconicity by definition. When
I speak, on the other hand, I can repeat a word to indicate
the plural (at least if I'm speaking Indonesian: *orang-orang*

means "two people"), or else, for emphasis, I can stretch out my vowels: whaaaaaat!, reeeeally? And that's not simply being colloquial, noooo, that's linguistic iconicity.

Or else I can make use of onomatopoeia, words that imitate or reproduce sounds, like animal calls—*meow*, *woof*, *moo*. Or even words related to sound, like *squawk*, or *murmur*, or *boom*. Every language has its special relationship to onomatopoeia. Italian is fairly limited. Japanese, meanwhile, is much more inventive: for example, a rolling object is a *korokoro* when it's light, but a *gorogoro* when it's heavy. You can almost hear them rolling with their two different weights, the repeated syllables signaling their continuous movement, regardless of how swiftly they're barreling forward. Now try testing your imagination: without checking the footnotes (no peeking!), what do you think a *tekuteku* might be?* Or a *pyonpyon*?† Both are words that suggest a clear and vivid image. Their sounds are "iconic"— and I don't mean "memorably famous," but iconic in the linguistic sense, *icon-based*, as I'll use the term throughout this book. (And by the way, I know you peeked!)

English is even more fertile ground. In the comic books I read as a little girl, Batman and Robin were always dispatching one villain or another, and in such striking, realistic ways I could almost feel their pain: CRASH! BANG! ARRRGH!—the fight balloons imitating the sounds of their flying fists. By dint of all these onomatopoeic blows, one of Batman's supervillains was even named Onomatopoeia. Iconicity leaves an incredibly strong impression, with enough impact to become a physical character. This strength, how-

---

* A brisk walk.
† A hop.

ever, is limited to the page. Imagine a film where the bad guy fires his gun and "BANG" pops out—he'd look like a fool (or, at least, like Jim Carrey in *The Mask*).

In the early stages of every invented script, the signs' iconicity played a powerful role (fig. 1). Or more than a powerful role—graphic iconicity served as the first true springboard for the invention of writing. In China, Mesopotamia, Egypt, Mesoamerica, and elsewhere, too, icons made themselves heard, pronouncing their names in a range of languages: Old Chinese, Sumerian, Pre-Pharaonic Egyptian, and Proto-Mayan.

1. Examples of iconic signs from the first scripts
(Egyptian hieroglyphs, archaic cuneiform, Nahuatl, Cretan hieroglyphs, Mayan, and Anatolian hieroglyphs)

But this is where our problems begin: How do we define the relationship between icons and symbols, which—unlike true icons—lack a clear, transparent, and recognizable meaning? And how do we account for abstractions?

SYMBOLS

Symbols are as old as mankind, and I don't mean *Homo sapiens*. As far back as the Paleolithic cave paintings from forty thousand years ago, alongside the naturalistic and "legible" depictions of animal icons, we find a series of abstract signs. And strangely enough they're the same signs that we find at other sites around the world from this same period, from the Lascaux and Chauvet caves in France to the island of Sulawesi in Indonesia to the Blombos Cave in South Africa, which dates back even further.

Surrounding the paintings of horses, bison, and faceless men are thirty-two geometric forms, simple but beautiful—circles, asterisks, zigzags and triangles, parallel lines, spirals, hands stenciled on the wall (fig. 2). The exact same forms, in different corners of the world. These aren't mere scribblings, but deeply moving and powerful signa-

2. Handprints in the Cueva de las Manos, Santa Cruz, Argentina

tures that mark one of the most important moments in the history of our species, like the invention of tools or the discovery of fire. They signal the desire, deeply ingrained in all of us, to say something, to bestow meaning, in whatever form, even with simple, erratic markings. Their power lies in their message: these traces will remain, long beyond the moment I steal from time to make them.

Whoever made these marks knew their meaning, too, since they were linking language and spoken expression to graphic creativity. They therefore constitute the first form of communicating abstract thought—even if for us, today, they remain unsolvable enigmas. Of course, they're not writing per se, but they do mark the first creative lunge in what was (I'd daresay) an all-but-inevitable direction.

We're a species that's dominated by symbols, and we're not always so sure of how to decipher them. Nor can we always reconstruct their origin and evolution. Where do they come from, why did we create them? What was the spark that gave rise to abstraction?

When we depict something precise, with a specific name, using an icon-image, we create a sign. These signs are often called "pictograms." The term is inaccurate and misleading, since a drawing, the moment it becomes the name for the thing represented, ceases to be a drawing. It becomes a sign. It's already a script in embryo.

I draw a cat's face. I call it "cat" and not "gatto" or "chat." I usher it into the linguistic realm of English. The cat becomes a logogram for my language. A sign referring to the English word *cat* and nothing else. The name acquires substance, the feline substance of an American cat.

I draw a foot. I call it "foot"—a logogram. I draw a foot, but this time to indicate the verb "to walk." I've abstracted the foot's materiality, and I've set it in motion. I've created something else—an ideogram—by toying with the geography of meaning. I've expanded its possibility, though I've also rendered the sign's meaning more obscure. I've made a marvelous, irresistible mess.

How did we get to this point? To the man and woman figures on restroom doors, to traffic signs, the buttons on a washing machine, music notes, all the things we interpret daily just to get by in the world? From the geometry of an object's lines to our imaginative manipulation of meanings, we play with the nature and life of symbols each and every day. And most of the time, as we'll see, we even enjoy ourselves.

Let's turn back now to our two overarching stories. The first story I'll tell is pervaded by the scent of the sea—along with the aroma of three ingredients that affect us in powerful ways, engaging our intellect, our logical skills, and our intuition. All three challenge us to understand one another more deeply and truly. They help us to better see the world, to recognize and reorganize the data we absorb from our environment, and to piece it all together.

They are mystery, competition, experiment.

UNDECIPHERED
SCRIPTS

Islands

In our first story, mystery, competition, and experiment are all tied to islands. This despite the often warped ideas we hold of islands in general: ancestral eco-paradises, idyllic, primordial worlds, with their vibrant, violent, indomitable flora, and civilization nowhere near. Islands have long enticed us as realms of escape, a chance to get back to the simple life. They're lands that lend themselves to forgetting.

In our story, however, islands are the opposite: homes to complex society, often at the vanguard, sophisticated centers of creation and experimentation. Bustling hubs of inhabitants laboring to leave their trace. No time for kicking back. In our story, islands are nodes of invention and aspiration, affirmations of identity. The islands in this chapter are the seedbed of a profound human desire, one that perhaps lives in all of us: the urge to prove that we're unique.

This seems to be an essential ingredient in the scripts native to islands. Diversity accompanied—almost without fail—by enigma. In the world today there remain close to a dozen scripts that we still can't read or comprehend. They are indecipherable. And in this book we'll explore nearly all of them, from the Voynich Manuscript to the writing system developed in the Indus Valley, island-hopping our way around the world. And that's no mere turn of phrase, since nearly half of these undeciphered scripts were formed on islands: Cyprus, Crete, Easter Island. What is it that binds these (as of yet) uncracked codes from far-flung lands? Mere chance? Or is there, at root, some logical explanation?

Mystery and creativity, secrecy and innovation, diversity and competition. But we're still missing that third element: on islands, too, writing is an attempt, an experiment. And in the relentless avalanche of history, this attempt—at least in the long run—often comes to nothing. As we'll learn, it's almost as if there's something incomplete about the soul of islands, something sketched, unfinished. The creative flair flickers and goes out. Very few island scripts end in success. Neither for themselves, since they vanish, nor for us, still unable to penetrate their enigmas.

And yet every single one of these scripts possessed a tenacious will to exist, to resist. Where they often went wrong was in remaining local, refusing to seek vital nourishment elsewhere, to roam into distant territories. Their obstinate urge to live stretched no farther than their sea-lapped shores.

Perhaps the only way to survive, when you're on a perfect Eden, is to walk away from it.

Crete

Undeciphered. A code unbroken. Crete left us four scripts: Cretan Hieroglyphic, Linear A, the Phaistos Disk, and Linear B. Only one, the last, have we managed to interpret. How is that possible? How is our knowledge so limited? How could it be that we understand so little about this island's languages? Is four thousand years all it takes to bury the whole lot of us in silence?

FACE FORWARD

There's far too much about our origins that we still don't understand. Languages, names, migrations, cultural encounters. Without a deciphered, comprehensible script in hand, we remain cut off from the richness and particularity of the details. Archaeology can help us to understand ways of life, styles, cultural preferences, the material things. The mind, however, gifts us the exactitude of thought.

It sounds like a paradox, but the more thoroughly we here in Europe explore our own backyard, the less we understand. The very first scripts to emerge on this old continent are its most impenetrable forts. Insurmountable walls stand between us and the secrets of our origins. Who invented the first European script? Which language (or languages) did it record? In other words, and in short, where do we come from?

The concept of Europe is of course a historical construct, composed of various layers of occupations, heritages, traditions, and a fair share of mystification. The European identity has long been celebrated and scorned in equal measure, because its borders are fickle, its colors too faint. Digging back through millennia to piece together a sense of identity is no easy task, because identity is a fluid, changeable thing. Questions of "belonging" are always a source of dispute. And often, rather than embrace this complexity, we assault it, precisely because it rests on shaky ground. We're in desperate need of roots.

So where do we turn, if we're looking to claim some sense of kinship? As Greek myth and its ideal geography would have it, the first place to search is Crete, given that the mother of the island's King Minos bore the name Europa. Europe is Crete, Crete is Europe, from the dawn of time, on the wings of fable. Roots.

The Ancient Greek language throws in a hand, too: *eurys*-, "wide," *ops*-, the root for "face" (though this etymology may have been drummed up to make the name more comprehensible). Europe and its wide gaze on the world, overseeing all, from Greece onward. Still others contend that the name is Semitic in origin, tying it to the West: *ereb*, all that looks westward.*

I guess that means it's face forward, then, eyes fixed on the Occident. Except our eyes are closed, since we still don't know with any certainty where we come from. Europe the shapeshifting concept, a continent with no clear sense of its

---

* Providing artificial interpretations for the names of people and places: a favorite creative pastime among the more cavalier philologists.

original languages, and all of us Europeans the result of a dubious concoction of cultures.

Even Homer spoke of Crete as a cultural melting pot, resounding with a jumble of different languages. He puts this in the mouth of Ulysses, who lets on to poor Penelope that he's the descendant of Minos himself. Crete, he tells her, is filled with countless peoples, countless cities, languages on languages—Achaeans, Eteocretans, Kydonians, Dorians, Pelasgians. But who are all these peoples?

Let's fumble around in the dark a bit, though not without some optimism. If Crete is the dawn of Europe, aren't we bound, someday, to catch a glimmer of hope? And where else but in the Cretan texts that we still don't know how to read?

PIONEERS

Let's start here, then, from Crete. Let's start from the beginning. We're in a four-thousand-year-old cemetery. In the middle of the Mediterranean's fifth-largest island, after Sicily, Sardinia, Cyprus, and Corsica. Once again, its name is charged with mystery: Crete. We're not sure where it comes from, perhaps an ancient Anatolian dialect, *kursatta*, meaning "island"—an instance of antonomasia.*

Which would mean that Crete wasn't just any old island, but *the* island. Though let's not lend it too much importance: it also feels like the kind of name that someone who hasn't seen very many islands might come up with. Imagine an Anatolian used to seeing Samos or Mytilene. Crete

---

* The asterisk here indicates that we're in the realm of reconstruction, therefore the realm of the unknown.

would seem like an enormous continent. Crete = Europe, like a continent. But how does Anatolia factor into this? It's now commonly believed that Crete, thousands of years ago, was slowly but inexorably colonized by Anatolian migrants. Our chaotic melting pot, with all its unthinkable fusions. But more on that in a second.

On the tombs in this cemetery are seal stones made of bone—tiny, intricately carved. An exquisite example of miniature art. Here we have the first European inscriptions. And they're strange. Some of the signs are familiar: a double axe, a vase. Others are abstract already—it's not clear what they represent. The seal stones were designed to stamp clay nodules, but they were precious objects. Objects that may have been used solely for display, to indicate one's social status, later to be buried in the tomb along with other status symbols—a fly-shaped pendant, an Egyptian musical instrument. "Pay attention to us," these objects plead.

The dead in the cemetery at Archanes speak to us of their wealth, their intelligence, their exclusivity. They manipulate signs. They write down a phrase, a sacred formula perhaps, and they repeat it. There are only a handful of seal stones, but they all bear the same five signs. And it's not just any phrase. It's a mantra that will enjoy a long history on the narrow stretch of island that is Crete. The dead of Archanes know how to distinguish themselves from others. They know how to compete, to experiment. They are pioneers.

AS GOOD AS NEW

In this fertile ground, Europe's first script takes root. Scripts, in the end, account only for so much. The years pile up. Nowadays there's a European Parliament with a very different set of problems to confront. But how fascinating it would be to roam the linguistic labyrinth of the so-called Archanes formula, to explore its five signs, to grasp just how these icons and symbols were chosen and transformed into a meaningful phrase, an important message, a group's identity—untouchable, solemn, sacred.

It's from these five repeated signs that we made our way to the first full-fledged script. But how did we get there? What did Minos's Cretans have in mind at the outset of their creation? An invention from scratch? A spin-off of Egyptian hieroglyphs? Did the Cretans draw inspiration from Egyptian culture, already nearly a thousand years old? Were they copycats? Or did they look around and draw upon their own environment, their own objects, tuning in to the sound of their own cognitive gears? Which is to say, did they act upon a true flash of intuition, with no outside help? Did they invent?

We still have no clear answers to these questions. But that hardly matters. The writing system that grows out of the Archanes formula is as good as new. We call it Cretan Hieroglyphic but it's nothing at all like Egyptian hieroglyphs. New signs, new symbols, new palaces erected along the shores. The mythical Minos, with his labyrinth and his sacred bulls, Minos the pioneer of the Cretans, ruling over all from the palace of Knossos, scanning the sea with his "wide" gaze (Europe!). He's already cosmopolitan, our Minos. He can write, and he invents a formidable script.

But the Cretan Hieroglyphic script is not hieroglyphic. We refer to it as such only because we suffer from Egyptian imprinting—and it's a misleading model. Hieroglyphic means nothing more than iconic, figurative, image-based. Like all writing systems throughout the world that have been poorly defined as hieroglyphic (from Mayan to Anatolian), it's a system that relies on clear reference points, signs that are recognizable at first sight: eyes, legs, hands, pots, plants. Other signs are considered abstract, geometric, linear.

And this iconicity is of great interest to us. Understanding it will help us pry open the stubborn window onto our origins. And it's a topic we'll revisit, since it points to why drawings played such an important role as a springboard to writing's invention.

HOUSE OF CARDS

The expression *seal the deal*, as we know, means to make a pact, reach an agreement, conclude a negotiation, to seal it shut. In Crete, sealing transactions was more important than writing poetry. Cretan hieroglyphs are found almost exclusively on bureaucratic documents. There is no literature, no fiction, no science. There are no stories or histories. A small, elite group of citizens functioned as palace managers, overseeing all agricultural and industrial production. Little else mattered to them, in these mini-states with maximum bureaucracy.

And they enjoyed creating objects in miniature, like seal stones, just as their recent predecessors had done in Archanes, following in the same tradition: tiny, intricate, highly skilled relief carvings. And signs. The first signs of a bona fide European writing system. Language, fixed in place at last.

These seal stones offered very little room—enough for brief formulas, which often appeared in similar sequences and may have been used to indicate the bureaucracy's top officials and their various roles. The unrepeated words might then have been the officials' names, but these are only guesses, however well informed. In a way, the seals were a kind of functional, personalized gemstone. A valuable ID card.

The engraved seals were made of colored semiprecious stones, in a prism or pendant shape, which were worn around the neck like amulets, or as charms on a bracelet. For whoever wore them, they were a symbol of power, signaling that person's ability to read and write and their important administrative role. As well as helping them to stand out among the crowds that gathered around the palaces, during ceremonies, at banquets.

Upon entering a palace, one walked through halls and rooms frescoed with scenes of processions, religious symbols, dancing figures. Then on into the grand courtyard, where a large but select group would gather. The who's who of Minoan society were easy to spot—the women with their flowing, ornate skirts, their breasts exposed, wearing gaudy golden jewelry. We have fewer depictions of the men, which should by no means lead us to envision a matriarchy or some early strand of feminism (a conclusion as bold as it is unfounded). The seal stones were a bit like our modern-day business cards, ivory card stock printed with fancy fonts and flourishes. The intellectual set flaunted their seals, though their function was more or less the same—to legitimize one's role in society, facilitate trade, ratify a proposed transaction. To keep everything under control.

And this control extended beyond the material—it was tied to perception. For the Minoans, as for us, appearance was fundamental: the upper classes were required to wear the proper clothes, adhere to the latest trends, plaster the walls of their homes with elaborate frescoes. Visiting a palace was not so different from the way we aspirationally scroll through Instagram or window-shop online, spending hours on Net-a-Porter without actually buying anything. Climbing the social ladder was, as ever, strictly tied to conspicuous consumption. And the result? The proliferation of a "palace style."

In the Cretan culture of four thousand years ago, bureaucracy reigned all but supreme. Though the instruments used to practice it, like writing, also carried a notable symbolic and personal significance. Engraving your name on a precious object, leaving your signature, distinguishing yourself in public—these were all meticulously curated strategies. Owning a seal with your name imprinted on it held much more appeal for the upper classes than, say, wearing a signet ring with your family crest does today, since Minoan seals were both a sign of your social position and a functional object, used to stamp important documents. Mini-monuments to status, wielded by the attentive landlords of a palatial housing complex.

STRAY CAT

When you think of the Minoans, what images come to mind? The labyrinth, the Minotaur, bull-leaping, perhaps? Do you remember the myth of Pasiphaë, Circe's mystical and unfaithful sister? Pasiphaë was Minos's wife, punished by Poseidon for neglecting to offer him a sacrificial bull. Not just any bull, of course, but the most beautiful bull in the world, with a hide as white as snow. Her punishment comes as a kind of Dantean *contrappasso*: Pasiphaë falls victim to the charms of the bovine hunk. And to help her satisfy her desire, the architect Daedalus builds her a wooden cow disguise. The queen commits a beastly act of adultery. Thus is born the Minotaur, a ferocious hybrid of a creature, who winds up trapped in the labyrinth. The bull is also central to the myth of the rape of Europa, Minos's mother, violated by Zeus in the guise of (what else but) a bull.

Minoan bull, Greek bull, the image keeps turning up, because the Minoans find a place for it wherever humanly possible: in palaces, in houses, their walls covered with monumental horns and bucrania, scenes of bull-leaping, miniature calves. Crete is littered with real and metaphorical horns.

But cats, on the other hand . . . In Cretan iconography, cats hold a special place. Not something to constantly show off, like bulls, no. They're a very different kind of protagonist, of a more, well, feline subtlety. In palace frescoes they figure as predators, though the scenes evoke the pastoral peace of a pleasure hunt—the cats are shown trotting around, almost playing with the birds and pheasants they should instead be pursuing. Even the famous Minoan "snake goddess," though she bears knifelike serpents in both of her hands, has a cat on her head. I'm not kidding—she wears a cat on her head like a trophy.

It's on seal stones, however, that cats really come into their own. There, amid writing symbols, we find them with their tails curled up and their big eyes bulging open, as if sketched by Walt Disney himself (fig. 3). Carved with a lathe into the seal's surface, they seem like a beautiful decoration, exotic almost, unmoving. And mute. Though, as we'll discover, their sound can still be heard.

For years and years, these engraved cats were mistaken for a design element. But they're no mere decoration, no simple frill. They're a sign, through and through.

The cat has a long history in Crete. We find it on the clay tablets of yet another Cretan writing system—it, too, like

3. A jasper seal stone, carved with Cretan hieroglyphs,
including a cat (first on the left)

Hieroglyphic, undeciphered: Linear A. Linear A is a syllabary with some ninety signs, along with an almost infinite
series of logograms. That two very similar writing systems
were created and used on the same island, in more or less
the same period, is nothing short of remarkable. In fact,
the two scripts even overlap: Linear A and Hieroglyphic
coexisted on the island for nearly two centuries, though we
don't have a clear sense of their "kinship"—whether they
record the same language or two different languages. That
said, the two systems are similar at the graphic level. Their
signs look alike. And they may have even more in common
than we think, though that will require more research. In
one aspect, however, they're markedly different: the seals.
When carved into seals, Cretan Hieroglyphic is almost always limited to icons. When writing on clay, on the other
hand, everything changes: the signs become slender, angu-
lar. Linear, in other words. And here Linear A has the upper hand. It's precisely this linearity that will bring Linear
A its success: over time, Cretan Hieroglyphic dies out on
its own. It is supplanted, substituted, absorbed. Lines and
their simplicity win the day.

And such is the destiny of our cat—to become linear, ten-
uous, schematic: the skeleton of a cat (fig. 4), as we find it on

4. The evolution of sign A80 (the syllable *ma*) in Linear A

Linear A tablets. So bare-bones did the symbol become over time that tracing it back to its origin—the cat icon featured on seal stones—proved to be an undertaking. Academics tend to entrench themselves in their own ideas: once something is defined as a drawing, it stays a drawing. Which was precisely the problem with Egyptian hieroglyphs, before Champollion broke the code: "It's not writing," went the mantra, "they're only drawings." And the same again with Mayan glyphs: just drawings. When meanwhile the key—the road to finally deciphering them—was right there in the signs' iconicity.

It's time we restore dignity, then, to the cat's *meow*. On seal stones a cat corresponds to the syllable *ma*. We know this because we find the same sign in Linear B, which descends (as its name so unimaginatively suggests) from Linear A—though unlike A, B has been deciphered. In Linear B the syllable *ma* is linked to the image of a feline, here represented by a grossly simplistic sketch of a cat's snout. Only the most essential elements remain. Poor cat, indeed, but a miraculous feat of distillation. A coup of contour. The human mind is made up almost entirely of images. But sounds, too. We're visual *and* auditory creatures, remember?

Across many of the world's languages, we find one splendid thing in common. It's surely an outlier case, but the sound made by a cat is almost always represented in the same way. This won't work with other animals. An English rooster goes *cock-a-doodle-do* and an Italian one *chicchirichì!* A Russian dog goes *gav* and an Indonesian one *guk*. Cats, on the other hand, are universal: they can *meow* in English, *miao* in Italian, *meo* in Vietnamese, *myau* in Russian, and so on and so forth. The differences are minute. This is true (incredibly!) for ancient languages, too. And by now you probably get what I'm driving at.

If I were a Minoan cat—with my beautifully open and simplified syllables, nearly all consonant-vowel pairs, as in Linear B (and Linear A)—what noise would I make? If I were a Minoan cat, I'd go *ma*. A resounding *maaaaa*, then, in the face of all the Minoan bulls that roamed the palaces.

SYLLABLES

It's time now we clear up a few things about the most important element in language: the syllable. There's something mysterious about syllables. Do you ever find yourself dwelling on the syllable as an inexhaustible source of mystery? Not likely. Nobody in their right mind thinks that way—but I do. And I'm not alone. I can still picture one of my old professors—her pencil lodged (invariably) between her teeth, her dusty, frumpy skirt, her air of utter pitilessness: "For a linguist, the syllable is one of the hardest things to describe." Those were the days.

But the fact is, she was right. If I say *huh*, we can all agree that it's one syllable, but so is *strengths*, with its nine letters. Like the word *vowel* with its deceptive vowels, the syllable is a slippery entity. Yet our very ability to communicate relies on it.

At the root of all this is a biomechanical issue: we open our mouths gradually wider when we pronounce vowels and regulate the flow of their sound. The longer we hold the vowel, the more forceful it becomes. If you open the window and scream *stooooooooop*, the force of the sound is sustained by that extended *oooooo*. (Texans, with their characteristic drawl, know a thing or two about this.)

Primates do the same thing. They use warning calls. They open their mouths and vocalize. They're able to make themselves understood, to give directions—but these sounds remain strictly vocalizations, because they're too rigid and exact: they don't combine to create compositions, they don't extend beyond what they are. And that's precisely where our expressive capacity lies: we know how to combine small entities of sound into complex architectures like words or grammar. And then we throw in one extra element: a symbolic meaning. By symbolic I mean nonindexing (sound + alarmed gazelle = a leopard is approaching, a fixed expression that indicates one thing and one thing alone); I mean fluid, free, divorced from context.

The words *beware* and *leopard* work well together in the moment of alarm, when danger strikes your safari tour, but their individual expressive potential, as words taken on their own, can be reconfigured and reconstructed elsewhere. They're open-ended. We humans hate closed circles, communicative short-circuits; we've learned to play pretty well with the Lego blocks of expression. Each of these blocks is a syllable. And that's where it all happens— whether it's the moment we start doubling up syllables and repeating *ma ma* and *pa pa*, at around twelve months old, or the moment we invented the first writing systems (all syllabic), around five thousand years ago. The syllable is of staggering importance in our desire to express ourselves, whether in speech or in writing.

That humanity ever landed upon the alphabet (in which each unit of sound corresponds to a single letter) was a matter of sheer good fortune, a cultural epiphenomenon, an unlikelihood of incredible consequence. The ancient Greeks cleared the way for their vowels (in a sea of Phoenician consonants), and thus created a democratic and economic product, destined for a success that was never guaranteed. But the alphabet is nothing more than an artifice, a brainy, sophisticated thing, like democracy or philosophy. We think in syllables, communicate in syllables, sing in syllables, and it was in syllables that we invented writing.

LOST LANGUAGE?

> O fortunate Crete!
>
> —*Idomeneus, King of Crete,*
>   Wolfgang A. Mozart (for the music, at least)

Not all Cretan syllables are so mysterious. Earlier I mentioned Linear B—let's talk about it, at least for a bit. The truth is, Linear B isn't of all that much interest to us, since it's been deciphered. For now, we'll spare it only a few measly lines. Though we'll come back to it, I promise, since it'll be of help when we look at the process of deciphering scripts.

So then, Linear B. This script records a very archaic Greek dialect, more than three thousand years old—the period during which the (so-called) Mycenaean palaces were in control of continental Greece and part of the island of Crete. Which meant that in Crete, after Cretan Hieroglyphic and Linear A, they (also) spoke a form of Greek, and they wrote using a syllabary, Linear B, not the Greek alphabet (still long from being adopted).

We know that Linear B records the Greek language because an English architect, Michael Ventris, deciphered it in 1952. It remains the first and only case of "internal decipherment," based solely on a statistical analysis of the script's signs, with no reliance on bilingual or trilingual texts.

For instance, both the Rosetta Stone and the cuneiform inscriptions of Persepolis include texts written in languages that are far better known: without the sections in Greek on the Rosetta, and without the Old Persian in Persia, we'd have had a much more difficult time reading Egyptian hieroglyphs and Babylonian, respectively. Having a little "outside" help makes life much easier. But with Linear B, miraculously, there was no need. And it's also the first case where the results are well established, and not the fruit of linguistic imagination and delusions. That Linear B has been deciphered is now an agreed-upon fact.

(Unlike with the Phaistos Disk and the Voynich Manuscript [which we'll look at later], both the subject of a steady stream of emails in my in-box, their authors eagerly pressing me for my advice or my backing. What these decipherers à la page all have in common is their presumption: never are their claims to have deciphered this [or that] script accompanied by a request for me to critique or disprove their method. They want only ratification. Which is why even we industry insiders proceed with caution. We'll soon see how finicky, fussy, and fastidious the work is for those who study undeciphered scripts—the daily grind of counting signs, checking and rechecking the data. A great way to lose your eyesight, it turns out, along with a neuron or two.)

So what to do, in the end, with the Aegean scripts from Crete that remain undeciphered, Cretan Hieroglyphic and Linear A? What hope do we have of following in Michael Ventris's footsteps and producing some real results?

There are many possible paths, and we'll get a closer look at them when we talk about decipherment techniques. Likewise, there are just as many doubts, which I bear with pride. There's only one thing I'll say with certainty. Our work, today, has one competitive advantage that has long been undervalued: a collaborative spirit. Toward Crete, for the love of the search, as Thales said. Together, I'd add.

Forget the lone individual on a hunt for glory. Collaboration is at the root of every modicum of progress ever gained, whether that door was opened with a battering ram or with the elegance of a carefully cut key. The wall that stands between us and interpreting, understanding, and embracing the first European languages, in the end, will fall. And even if the languages hidden behind Cretan Hieroglyphic and Linear A seem lost to us now (or perhaps just one language, equally lost?), no one can deny us the hope that we'll one day find them. Ancient languages we can reconnect with, like old friends. Or unknown languages, which we must labor to reconstruct.

Let us wish just one thing for ourselves, in the meantime—with a poetic, not a scientific, spirit, for a change: that their sound prove enrapturing, as full and fluid as music. Which is just how I hear it in my imagination or on sleepless nights: as rich with emotion as the Cretan chorus in Mozart's opera *Idomeneo*—named for the king of Crete, grandson of Minos. A tale with a happy ending. A fortunate tale. And a chorus, not a lone voice.

Cyprus

MIXTURES

The time has come to sail from Crete, even if we'll soon be back, to explore one of its most famous mysteries, the Phaistos Disk. For now, though, let's hop islands. We don't have far to travel. Welcome to Cyprus—island of everyone, island of no one.

It's hot here. You can see the Troodos Mountains in the distance, rolling down toward the sea, the land red with copper and iron, the sun pitiless and harsh, even in February, with snow still spattered on the mountain peaks. There's the smell of cypress in the air, cypress and dust.

I'm here to view the Cypro-Minoan tablets, to photograph them, study them, catalogue them. For months, I'll fly back and forth. And in the end, I'll write a book. It's 2012. It feels good to escape to Crete—Italy, where I've returned after nearly twenty years in England, seems more like a half relative, a stepmother, a place I cling to in search of roots.

As anyone who does research for a living knows, to stay put is in some ways to surrender, an almost passive act. A researcher must be mobile, ready to leave, to follow the current, slip from the confines of stability. I know this is subjective—there are certainly researchers who stay in one place—but for me, at least, research and travel are synonymous.

I leave with a precise aim: to see the Cypro-Minoan inscriptions and, while I'm there, to take in the smell of lemons, which in Cyprus are bitter and ubiquitous. Cyprus is a land of strong smells, the smell of borders, sand, and asphalt, a scent I've known for years now. It's both sleep-inducing and violent. The rhythm of life decelerates, but violence stirs in the air like a fine dust, on this island conquered by all, colonized one day, liberated the next, and still divided.

Divisions make little sense in general, but this is even truer in Cyprus, which has always been a melting pot: of ethnicities, colors, religions, foods, all in an ordered disorder. Cyprus runs on its own logic—it's a functioning Greece, so they say.

Cypriot vocabulary is littered with English and Turkish terms, a Greek dialect with a mixture of archaic sounds and pleasant, rounded sounds, which seem to dance between the tongue and the roof of the mouth. The coffee there is tagged with various adjectives: it's Turkish, or Cypriot, or Greek, or Arab, but it's always the same coffee, a thick brew made in a small long-handled pot called an *mbrikia*, allowed to sit and form a sediment, bitter as lemons. And Cyprus has many languages, too, which have been spoken there over the centuries. In modern times, a Greek dialect, and Turkish; in antiquity, a different Greek dialect, mixed with Phoenician, though still distinct, each with its own writing system.

If we dig even deeper into the past, we find what is perhaps an even more ancient language, in a secluded enclave: Eteocypriot. *Eteos*, meaning "true" Cypriot. The mother tongue. Very few inscriptions are preserved from the first millennium BCE, or nearly 2,500 years ago. We can read the Eteocypriot language because it was written using a Cypriot syllabary, known as the classical Cypriot syllabary (or Cypro-Greek), which in the same period also recorded a local Greek dialect, Arcado-Cypriot. One script for two languages, then—one Greek and the other clearly not. The mother tongue appears to be unknown: so what's going on here?

To make sense of it, we must travel even farther back in history, to 3,500 years ago—a time when the island was vibrant and prosperous, with urban centers on its shores and a geopolitical system under which no person ranked above any other. A heterarchy, with power divided up equally, and where the island's abundant copper (which in Latin was *aes cuprum*, derived from the name of the island itself) was a valuable trade resource throughout the eastern Mediterranean. The Minoan Cretans, who were expanding across the Aegean as far as the coast of Anatolia, seem to have made frequent visits to Cyprus as well, even if in their passing they left very few traces of their culture. One of these traces is their writing system. The Minoans' Linear A was adopted to record the Cypriot language, and perhaps one other language as well. The Cypriot language and the Minoan script melded together, and the resulting mixture was Cypro-Minoan. The script of the island of everyone, the island of no one.

1-2-3

I mentioned the possibility that Cypro-Minoan might be the script of more than one language. It's still up for debate.

In the 1970s, this was the theory in vogue among the few scholars in the world who studied it: Cypro-Minoan represents not one script but three. They based their evidence on the fact that some inscriptions seemed to have signs that were absent in other inscriptions, and seemed to be written in a different way. Examples of these divergent signs are found on four tablets.

(And I don't mean four tablets, give-or-take. I mean *only* four tablets—two of which, it should be noted, were glued together. So four tablets, then; three if you count this collage [fig. 5].)

In short, these four tablet fragments were set aside in their own group: the way they're inscribed seems to be a departure from all other inscriptions (CM 1), so it makes sense to call them by a different name (CM 2). We then take all of the inscriptions found outside Cyprus, which are also rare, and give them a third name (CM 3). There you have it, 1-2-3. Three subgroups of the same writing system. I should be diplomatic here, but it's a pretty illogical

5. The four tablet fragments inscribed with Cypro-Minoan

breakdown, is it not? I find it all perplexing. And I'm not the only one.

All in all, this script currently amounts to fewer than three hundred inscriptions. To break it down into different subgroups is counterintuitive. Nevertheless, in academia as in politics, *divide and conquer*. Never mind the fact that this 1-2-3 breakdown implies that we're dealing with three different languages, one for each of the script's subgroups.

This fragmentation, in recent years, has sparked a revival of scholarly interest. It's a kind of giant brain teaser, fueled by the most powerful question a scholar can ask: What if we're wrong? Our trusty scientific method—we test the hypothesis. Applied to Cypro-Minoan, this question translates to "What if this breakdown isn't helping?" A critical mass of scholars is now on the case. And it's about time.

In the end, it may simply be that Cypro-Minoan only *appears* to be three different scripts. Given how varied it is, inscribed on a host of different materials—silverware and bronzeware, golden jewelry, ivory plaques, clay objects— perhaps the markings vary in accordance with the material on which they're being made? It also seems that there were several different "scribes," each with their own handwriting—different people writing in different styles. As if the script were not standardized, regulated by a central bureaucracy. Perhaps Cypro-Minoan was just a bit "freer"?

And therefore different from the inscriptions found in Minoan and Mycenaean palaces. In Cyprus, they wrote *freestyle*, no bureaucrats to speak of. Failing to take this freedom into account is an error commonly made by scrupulous, and biased, scholars, who merely want confirmation of things they're already familiar with, like the palaces and their ordered and uniform tablets. Just because the model for the writing system in Cyprus is blatantly Minoan doesn't necessarily mean that the modus operandi is Minoan as well. Let's face it: the Cypriots, in the end, proud and diverse as they are, have always gone their own way.

Must we proceed with caution, then? We have no choice. Cypro-Minoan remains undeciphered, therefore no one can say precisely how many scripts, or how many languages, it represents. But the suspicion that the number is one, not three, is worming its way ever deeper into the morass of scientific publications in the field. We'll pick up the discussion again in the chapter on decipherment. For now, we'll have to withhold our judgment.

MINE

One thing we do know for sure: Cypro-Minoan was never used for management purposes. In this aspect, it differs greatly from the Aegean world. The Cypriot tablets, though few, bear extensive texts: they appear to be narrative in nature, not inventories of goods and products. This is highly interesting, and it confirms the fact that, though the Cypriots of the Bronze Age did indeed adopt another culture's writing system, they employed it to their own ends, which were by no means the economic tab-keeping of what we might call the Minoan Federation or the Cretan Ministry of State Property. That these somewhat tedious affairs were dealt with on different materials, such as parchment or papyrus, and that they never made it down to us—due precisely to the perishability of those materials—is another matter entirely. But we're much more practical than that. We have no interest in building hypotheses on the basis of invisible materials.

Let's try an imaginary experiment (or somewhat imaginary, anyway). Say we have before us an undeciphered script. A few odd inscriptions that we can't understand, recording what may be one or several languages. What can we draw from these mute texts, and from the script's subgroups, 1, 2, and 3, which we can't even catalogue? The prospects aren't exactly rosy. You can't squeeze blood from a turnip, as my grandmother would say. Nevertheless—and still quoting my grandmother—the beauty of imagination is that you can try to understand even without knowing how to read. Using your common sense, of course.

Shall we give it a shot? Let's give it a shot. Let's pretend we're Agatha Christie, on the trail of an elusive killer.

CLUE 1: Cypro-Minoan is written—engraved, painted, inscribed—on an incredible variety of objects, as we've noted. Metals, clay, ivory, earthenware pots. Nearly all of these objects are culturally significant and crafted with attention to aesthetic detail: ("beautiful," we'd call them, but beauty is a murky concept; best not to project it on the tastes of the ancients). In any case, we're not talking about commonly used tools or utensils.

CLUE 2: Writing is added to valuable objects to lend even more value to those who possess them. Doing so gives one a competitive advantage in society. This phenomenon is invariably linked with the desire to be seen. My object is embellished with something as rare and precious as writing (just like me, right?). Excuse my slang, but I want to be clear here: writing is rare and reserved for the few, and is therefore a way of making an object more badass. What's missing from my beautiful golden ring? Why, only that final, badass touch: i.e., an inscription.

CLUE 3: And what will my inscription say? You've probably already guessed it . . . it's so banal. What else would it say except that this object belongs to me. It's not yours, not public property, it doesn't belong to the local or central government. It is mine and mine alone. Hands off!

Three clues make for a good start, but there are still other facts we can glean. Let's take a look at the texts on these precious objects. They're brief, a few words at most, since it's hard to fit an epic poem with three hundred lines of blank verse on the side of a pot. Now look a bit closer. Some of the sequences conclude with the same sign. And that sign can mean only one thing, since it appears as the final word with remarkable consistency. What is it? It probably indicates property, to whom the object belongs, the name of its owner: "This ring belongs to Tom, or Dick, or Harry." Anyone who wrestled with a little Latin in school knows that this is the genitive case, although we can't simply claim that the genitive exists in Cypro-Minoan, since we'd have to take it for granted that it's a language like Latin, with declensions and cases. Much safer, in fact, to assume that it's inflectional, like all Indo-European languages. But can we even claim that Cypro-Minoan is Indo-European? I wouldn't dare. *Giammai*, as my grandma would say—never ever!

What we *can* say is that this insistence on indicating one's ownership—literally branding the object—was a bit narcissistic. We have no trace of any Mycenaean or Minoan scribe attempting to leave their name on anything, not even a humble administrative document. Industry, not ego, was the obsession in the pre-Greek Aegean—the system of production, not social rank. Meanwhile, check out these Cypriots, well ahead of their time, attuned to public image, PR whizzes who know how to manipulate writing as if it were a status symbol. Personalizing their luxury goods, showing off. Who knows what they might have done with Instagram.

THE KING'S MARBLES

Cypro-Minoan was a game reserved for the elite, not the people. The people, in truth, have never had an easy time claiming space for themselves in the annals of history—and even when they manage it, they're always being overshadowed by the kings, the commanders, the names of note. In Cyprus, they had an even harder time. Getting a clear sense of what village life was like there is difficult, and the funnel only gets narrower—we find evidence of the elite in the cities, in their residences, in cemeteries, in the grand sanctuaries and grand workshops dedicated to the "god" copper. Copper was their only true source of wealth, their principal means of trade with the eastern Mediterranean, almost as if it were a form of money in a society with no market or currency.

Cypriots were born to be merchants—as they have been for nearly four thousand years now. They're expert traders. They're entrepreneurs. They know how to conduct business, to coordinate, to unite industry and power in order to take full advantage of their prized metal. Without copper, there's no bronze. So the Bronze Age, for the Cypriots, is first and foremost the Copper Age. They understood this perfectly—and they made sure to cash in on it. The "god" copper is sacred because it means industry, and industry means wealth.

This coordination, all in the name of copper, can be witnessed in their writing. As evidence, we have nearly one hundred fired clay spheres, all of roughly the same diameter (two centimeters), and all of which bear rather scant inscriptions—two words on average, often just one (fig. 6). The briefest of texts on the tiniest of spheres, and yet rivers of ink have been spilled in trying to understand them:

What could they have been? What was their purpose? Toy marbles? Weights? Votive tokens? Sling bullets? It's amusing to explore the many interpretations, to imagine all of the archaeological minds at work, their philological-neuronal gears turning in pursuit of the most elusive explanation. Think of all the energy and creativity expended on the strange case of these tiny Cypriot spheres!

6. Clay ball inscribed with Cypro-Minoan

I lean toward good old common sense. Look at the following figure of miniature soccer balls, used for drawing the tournament brackets in the Champions League (fig. 7). Now look back at the Cypriot balls. Are you catching my drift? Sorting! The simplest explanation is always the most persuasive, and oftentimes it's the only shoe that fits, like Cinderella's glass slipper. If these spheres were indeed used for sorting, what would be inscribed on them? Another lob of a question—soccer hadn't yet taken hold in Cyprus. Obsession with status was their preferred pastime.

The clay spheres were fired intentionally, to make them durable, to preserve them. Important stuff, here—no small beans. What, then, is more important than a noun? A proper noun? Precisely. Inscribed on the spheres were

7. Champions League draw

proper nouns or official titles, public appointments. The former designated that specific person, and no one else, a matter of exclusivity; the latter indicated that it was someone of importance, recognizable via their societal role. But what were these roles? And how can we be so sure that these were truly proper nouns?

Because we have the proof, says Agatha (me). On those "badass" objects that we discussed earlier, a few sequences show up repeatedly, and they include the sign of the "genitive" (indicating the owner). That same mark of possession is nowhere to be found on the clay balls, which might instead bear the equivalent of the "nominative" case, or the subject. When these spheres were dug up—at least in the city of Enkomi, the area of the island that has been most thoroughly excavated—they were found in religious and industrial contexts. We already know that the sacred and the industrial worlds were tied up in a kind of all-in-one complex of copper workshops and sanctuaries, meaning that the people named must have been active in that realm. Illustrious figures, at the tip of the social pyramid. A priest, a high-ranking official, a king?

Whether or not there's a king involved is hard to prove, but we're now convinced that at the very least we're dealing with the upper crust of Cyprus in that day. The members of this aristocracy would be sorted for the purpose of some kind of activity, perhaps religious, perhaps political. Whichever it was, we can't say with any certainty. But that it was a public event, an important event, an event of display, seems beyond question at this point.

Not so different from when we select the brackets for our modern-day soccer tournaments, or for March Madness. But there are ancient examples, too, such as in Magna Graecia and in Sicily two thousand years ago. The Cypriots, however, seem to have been the first. Sorry, Champions League. (Go, Cyprus!)

ALMOST THERE?

And go, Cypro-Minoan. Because if we manage to decipher any of the as-yet-undeciphered scripts, Cypro-Minoan is in the pole position. And here's why.

Do you remember Eteocypriot, the mother tongue of the first millennium BCE? We discussed how it is written using the classical Cypriot syllabary, which we have no problem reading. And though we still struggle to piece together the structure behind Eteocypriot, since so few texts have survived, we can however boast of one small success: we've recognized its "genitive." And its genitive seems to be precisely the same genitive that's used to indicate ownership in Cypro-Minoan inscriptions. Same case, same inflection, same function. Eteocypriot survived from the second to the first millennium BCE—and this mother tongue may well be the language hiding behind Cypro-Minoan.

That's all that I'll say for now.

Cypro-Minoan is not the first European script; if we don't count the Phaistos Disk (a black swan, as we'll see), it's the third chronologically, after Cretan Hieroglyphic and Linear A. Cyprus is no hermit's hideaway, it's a planet of "oriental-occidental" voices and aromas like no other. And it's bound to yield more surprises, with its distinctly Mediterranean mixture of ethnicities and scents, languages and sounds, lemons and coffee. And these surprises are just around the corner.

INTERMISSION

What's not around the corner, however, is the other end of the world. And before journeying halfway around the globe from the Mediterranean, I'd like first to pause for a digression. What I'd like to tell you about are three "i" words that I hold very dear: the first is *islands*, but that much you already know; the second is *ideas*, which sometimes come and sometimes don't; and the third is *INSCRIBE*, an acronym I'll explain to you here in a second.

Let's start with ideas—elusive, wavering, at times unfaithful, like lovers lost and confused in the landscape of their amorous possibilities. If you're stuck between chasing after a hesitant lover or a fleeting idea, the latter is always a safer bet.

I'll soon be off to chase them down on a private and deserted island. And I'm not talking about some radical chic vacation, but an experiment. My trip will be free, no taxes or hidden fees, and, more important, no frills. A Swedish entrepreneur offers up his home to groups interested in developing an idea in a place far from all civilization, with no electricity, no comforts beyond four walls and a roof over our heads, and, possibly, a refrigerator. One precious week of the year, the occasional hammock here and there, and a few square miles of Swedish greenery.

This is the island of ideas, and it can be reached only by a rowboat large enough for six people—leaving behind, back on land, the constructs of everyday life, the world and its practical matters, our clingy electronics, and all thought of obligation, in order to make room for a different, freer kind of thinking. A week to think in silence is a luxury (in this case luxury-free). I'll write and reflect on writing, and as a group we'll put our heads together and continue in our quest to decipher the world's undeciphered scripts.

Speaking of my group—I present to you INSCRIBE. We're financed by the ERC, the European Research Council, therefore by the European Commission, though I won't be receiving any kickback for having waxed poetic about Europe earlier. The grant I received was to fund a research group focused on the invention of writing. INSCRIBE is an acronym for Invention of Scripts and Their Beginnings. Our aim is to reconstruct writing's invention using an analytical method that draws on several different disciplines—linguistics, archaeology, anthropology, visual perception and cognitive studies, the Digital Humanities. One of our goals is to discover just how many times writing has been invented throughout history, since the precise number of inventions has not yet been clearly established.

But that's not all. Our team is also committed to deciphering the undeciphered languages you're already familiar with—Cretan Hieroglyphic, Linear A, Cypro-Minoan.

Beyond these Aegean scripts, we study two others that remain undeciphered, which may or may not have been invented from scratch: one is the Indus Valley Script, and the other is Rongorongo, from Easter Island.

And it's to this last script that we'll turn our attention now. Let's leave behind the frog puddle of the Mediterranean (to Plato we're "like frogs or ants around a pond") and brave the ocean. The calm and benevolent ocean.

Easter Island

> And the dead tree gives no shelter, the cricket no relief,
> And the dry stone no sound of water.
> —T. S. Eliot, *The Waste Land*

That anyone found it at all seems like a miracle, lost in the middle of nowhere as it is. More than two thousand miles from the coast of Chile. We leap the Pacific from Santiago on a five-and-a-half-hour flight.

Now imagine the first landfall, somewhere around 1000–1200 CE. According to myth, the island's first king, Hotu Matu'a, arrived from the other side of the ocean—the Polynesian Islands—with a handful of men and women on catamarans and canoes, and sixty-seven tablets covered with signs. There to welcome them was a vast and craggy coastline, three volcanoes, a triangular piece of land covered in windswept hills, and fishless waters stretching all around. Though they had no sense of it at the time, they were the final stroke in the colonization of our planet, the last to step foot on pure and virgin soil.

Palm trees and forests covered the island. Rainwater pooled in the craters of extinct volcanoes. Fresh water gushed from the earth. According to very recent studies, it

was around these crater lakes that the Polynesian colonizers first began constructing ahu, the stone platforms that
serve as the bases for their moai statues, clustering them
near the water. The statues, like standard-bearers, loom
along the horizon, personifications of the island's ancestors, marking the water sources, like the sentinels of a past
and present life. The uncorrupted guarantors of future life.

The entire planet—land, sea, sky—was concentrated
in those 63 square miles: to see it was "to see a world in a
grain of sand and heaven in a wild flower, hold infinity in
the palm of your hand." For its inhabitants, the island was
the center of the world—*Te Pito o Te Henua*, in the local
language Rapa Nui.

Detaching yourself from a Ptolemaic view of things can
be difficult. What else would it be spinning around, this
world of ours, if not us? To be pushed from center stage is
disorienting, vertigo-inducing. It knocks you out of sync
with the earth's natural motion—either we're the ful-
crum, or we're completely off axis. To make sense of the
space around us, to keep from going dizzy, we must think
of ourselves as the only fixed point, while everything else
is moving around us. Only then can we guard ourselves
against the baffling and alienating effect of infinity. It
makes sense, then, that the planet is riddled with "centers
of the earth," spread out across the continents, from Istan-
bul, Babylonia, and Arizona to Easter Island. Every stage is
a world, to misquote Shakespeare.

But mankind leaves a heavy footprint. From the moment the human beast set foot on the island, the face of
Rapa Nui was marred. Towering palm trees destroyed,
burned, uprooted to cremate the dead, to construct planta-
tions and canoes, to build the moai, and for a host of other
purposes we can't imagine. It may not have been the rats'

fault after all, as many books on the collapse of the island's civilization suggest. The egocentric stride of human beings is more than capable of doing the job. Deforestation set off an irreversible domino effect: erosion by wind and rain, agriculture in fits and starts, smaller and smaller harvests, famine, and perhaps (as oral accounts from the population attest) even cannibalism. A full gallop toward destruction. So it was that this center of the world, floating out in the far reaches of the ocean, became a patch of desolate earth.

Like space, time knocks us stupid when we step out-side the present moment. All in all, it took Easter Island less than a thousand years to reach ecological suicide. One thousand years, in the 4.5 billion years of life on this planet, is the blink of an eye, a hiccup, a gunshot, Usain Bolt's 100-meter dash. You turn and it's already over—and in the meantime, your own center of the earth has changed its face forever.

MIRACLE

Yet in this suspended fragment of time, in Bolt's 100 me-ters, in the beat of a heart or the blink of an eye, space opens itself up to surprise, to bated breath, to a reaffir-mation of life. This interval can generate creative tension, impulse, discovery. On Easter Island, this creativity found expression in an astounding visual culture. There are sym-bols engraved in the shoulders of the moai; monumental, magnificent petroglyphs carved into basalt and volcanic rocks; and wooden tablets, densely packed with a series of signs—the Rongorongo language.

Today only a few of these illegible tablets remain, and

all are held far from their island of origin. The scripts are written boustrophedonically. Boustrophedon is writing that "follows the path of the ox," as the word's Greek origin tells us—which is to say, every other line runs in the opposite direction, from right to left and then from left to right, in a kind of alternating zigzag. Rongorongo, however, makes things (and the lives of us decipherers) even more complicated, since it's written in reverse boustrophedon: the signs in the second line are upside down with respect to the first, forcing the reader to turn the tablet over every other line. Not only that, but the language is read from bottom to top. It sounds truly strange, but reading a text was meant to be a kind of advanced choreography.

We rely on both sources—the petroglyphs and the wooden tablets—to make sense of this whimsical gesture, to explain this impulse, and to help answer two outstanding questions.

Question one: Are we talking about an actual script here? It seems almost a miracle that something so complex and refined could have emerged from the "wasteland" of Rapa Nui. Detractors—and there are always a few—dismiss it as a kind of proto-script. For them, to claim this series of signs as anything else is inconceivable. Or no, maybe they were used as pretty stamps, to add color to fabrics, given how beautiful and decorative they are? Icons of men, women, stars, mountains, animals, and every sort of winged creature. How could these possibly add up to a written language?

Remember our feline friend from Minos, exiled to the land of "drawings" when it was really a sign? Here we are again. It's easy to lose sight of iconicity: distinguishing between drawings and signs is the giant pitfall hiding in all invented scripts. And the idea of invention brings us to our second question: Is Rongorongo a script invented from scratch? With no outside influence? Before diving into this second question we must tackle the first—and in that arena, we stand in strong opposition to the detractors. Rongorongo is, in the fullest sense, a script. And we can say this with certainty because the consistent structures that underlie the inscriptions make clear that a natural language is being recorded (and that these are not simply fanciful decorations).

The next logical step would have been to compile a list of all the signs—but that's where the train jumped the tracks. Just after the Second World War, different schools (Russian vs. German) dedicated themselves to the task, though without reaching any shared conclusions (it wasn't exactly a friendly environment). The main takeaway being that, in war, and without collaboration, you're bound to make a mess of things: far-flung and unfounded decipherments, the list of signs overrun with redundancies, inconsistencies, dubiously patched-together symbols. Seven hundred signs, never organized into a rational inventory—but that's where we are. The number of signs alone, though clearly inflated, tells us at the very least that Rongorongo is a syllabary, with a series of logograms. The process of streamlining and ridding this list of all redundancies is still ongoing, but we're working on it, and we're getting close. The end is within reach. In the meantime, we can flaunt our discovery that Rongorongo is a logo-syllabary, exactly like all the other scripts invented from scratch (except, as we'll see, Egyptian).

Which brings us back around to our second question, regarding invention. We must leap nearly three hundred years into the past, to the day when a group of Dutch sailors disembarked on the island. It was Easter Sunday, 1722. There to greet them was a treeless expanse, the earth parched, but the same craggy coastline and the same winds found by the first colonizing king, Hotu Matu'a. This crew, of course, did not come bearing any tablets.

What is the origin story, then, of Rongorongo? The miracle lies not only in the creation of a script in such an isolated place, but also in the possibility that this creation might have come from nowhere, from the ingenuity of the locals alone, and not from the influence of some hyperciv-ilized foreign colonizers. The miracle lies in the invention of something new and never before seen. A lantern flick-ing on, glowing between the craggy coasts, between the waves of wind and water. There are those who will never admit that such a thing is possible, but I'm not one of them. Invention is within everyone's reach—just as likely to be found between the magmatic folds of a volcanic island as it is in the crowds of a densely packed city. Invention is in our brains, lying dormant, around the corner, churning away while we're busy distracting ourselves with other matters.

And to be honest, it makes little difference if the in-habitants of Rapa Nui were in some vague way exposed to the Roman alphabet, or to the treaties of colonizers, or to the stew of European letters before they invented Rongorongo. The inhabitants of Rapa Nui—before they became victim to egregious and invasive abuses of power, before their civ-ilization was demolished—invented a writing system with completely new signs, one that had little to do with the ele-mentary European alphabet. That we're dealing with a new writing system, and therefore an invented writing system, is irrefutable. And don't forget that it's a logo-syllabary, like all scripts that have been invented from the ground up. Which means that its signs are iconic in form. Syllables, iconicity, uniquely formed signs—all are ingredients associated with the miracle of the inventive spark. In just a few pages we'll be able to provide more tangible proof (more tangible, at least, than my undeniable partiality) that what we have here is a true case of invention, if you're not yet convinced by the structural evidence. But first let's go back to the future, three hundred years later—to the present day, that is.

DODO'S EGG

We step into a quiet room, lit as if it really were a museum gallery. Father Alberto, of the Congregation of the Sacred Heart, is there to welcome us. We're in the north of Rome, on a nameless street—residential, deserted. We press the intercom button like we're paying a visit to old friends, and we're greeted with an espresso and an incredible story. Why are four of the twenty-six wooden tablets inscribed with Rongorongo in Rome, nearly ten thousand miles from their native island? What are they doing here?

Hidden behind display cases, guarded with equal doses of humility and pride, these tablets, Father Alberto tells us, were saved at the last minute by a group of missionaries. Just before the tablets were to be burned, the missionaries noticed the engravings covering them from end to end. "What are all these signs?" The Tahitian bishop Florentin-Étienne Jaussen was the first to bring fame to Rongorongo and to begin studying it. He saved the tablets and sailed them back to Rome at the end of the nineteenth century. And they've been here ever since, under careful watch.

Father Alberto takes immediate, passionate interest in

our cause. We're here with experts in geodesy and geomatics from INSCRIBE, whose aim is to collect 3D images, using an extremely powerful laser scanner, of all the undeciphered scripts that we study—the Aegean scripts (Cretan Hieroglyphic, Linear A, Cypro-Minoan), as well the Rongorongo tablets. We're starting out in our own center of the world, Rome, but we'll soon be chasing down inscriptions all over the globe, from St. Petersburg to Hawaii, not to mention Cyprus and Crete.

Our object of study today is the Mamari tablet (fig. 8). *Mamari*, in the language of Rapa Nui, means "egg," even if the tablet's shape is more circular than ovoid, with smooth and shiny edges. It's made of wood, with numerous signs carved into both sides, intricate and densely packed, each line engraved only lightly into the surface, each sign faint and elegant in its sinuous and well-proportioned form. From this description, the tablet seems merely beautiful—and beautiful it is—but it's also a nightmare for our scanner. In a sense, we're trying to enact our own little miracle: to use the most effective technology possible in order to create a three-dimensional model that captures the signs in all their detail, giving us the most accurate "reading" of the text. It's a task we've been laboring at for months.

Today is the decisive day, and it's time to celebrate, because we've produced a "passable" result. *Passable* is the adjective the engineers use to describe it. Translated into layman's terms it means "mind-blowing." A few words should be said about geodesists, who are a species unto themselves: they are expert engineers who create models for measuring the geometric shape of the earth and its gravitational field. They're temperate creatures, with their own reaction times and their own shared language, which I'm

8. The Mamari tablet, inscribed with Rongorongo

beginning to understand myself. They have a certain obsession with symmetry, order, and a balanced objectivity.*

Today is the first time I've seen them get emotional. Catching sight of a teary-eyed engineer is like finding a dodo's egg on the shores of Ostia Antica. Witnessing three of them, no less, with half-moon smiles and rows of teeth wide enough to stretch the earth's atmosphere, is like coming across a zoo full of dodos, alive and well.

And what will we do with these 3D models? Here's the plan: to create the first digital archive of every existing Rongorongo tablet. To bring them to you. To make it so that everyone, if only virtually, can access these tablets, can touch them, zoom in on them, flip them upside down like they're playing a video game. These models will help us to distinguish the exact form of each sign, down to the finest

---

* What's the difference between an introvert engineer and an extrovert engineer? The introvert looks down at his own shoes while he's talking to you; the extrovert looks down at yours.

detail, to reimagine just how they were inscribed into the wood. This is crucial to making sure that we have consistent word sequences, from which we can then reconstruct the language's morphological underpinnings (its grammar, in other words) and check to see if there are repetitions, logograms, numerals, etc.

Days like today are a source of immeasurable joy. Being able to read the signs properly is only the first step, yes, but it is without doubt the most important, the foundation of deciphering a writing system. Being able to recognize each sign, down to its finest detail, is the oboist's tuning note that will allow us to reconstruct the entire scale of sounds in Rongorongo. If that's not soul-stirring, I don't know what is. The key to interpretation is within reach. Now that you, that we, have seen the signs, we're left with the burden of finding proof that the script was an invention, as I noted earlier. To do so, we must return to the moai and take a closer look—at both sides.

WATCH YOUR BACK

From the earliest phases of construction, which date to around the very first wave of colonization, the moai proliferated and became the island's symbol. One thousand statues, gazing inland. So taken are we with these friendly giants—so visible are they, so exposed—that all other artistic works on the island, which are far more numerous, have been relegated to obscurity. Blame it on their reticent, guarded beauty—the kind that's harder to detect, the kind you recognize only much later, and only because you took a closer look. The petroglyphs, engraved in bas-relief or painted, are perhaps the true masterpieces of Easter Island.

At the crater of Rano Kau we find a narrative sequence of petroglyphs that stretches nearly ten feet—a swirl of sea creatures, a human-faced octopus, imaginary bird-fish (fig. 9). It looks like a mythic tale.

And there are other drawings that appear almost to have perspective, overlaid by figures of birdmen. These birdmen are everywhere, with their wide eyes and pointed beaks, their human bodies curled in the fetal position. Sacred and bellicose, they recall the strength of warriors, the matato'a. And they dominate the site of Orongo, at the rim's highest point, one of the triangular island's three corners, jutting perilously into the ocean. Here priests chanted for the annual egg hunt—in which the winner, who returned with the season's first egg, would be declared "birdman" for the year.

And then there are the sea creatures, anthropomorphic figures, turtles, birds, geometric motifs, that we find

9. An image of the "birdman" from Rapa Nui

engraved on the backs of the moai. These drawings are the precursors of the signs we find in the Rongorongo script. And here we must pay careful attention—we must concentrate on this art, we must contextualize it, in order to understand their writing system's origin. Properly dating the moai and the petroglyphs is crucial. They without doubt precede the birth of Rongorongo, by nearly half a millennium, but that's not evidence enough. The petroglyph symbols are remarkably similar to the signs in Rongorongo. Some are even identical.

This preexisting iconography seems to be the island's generative source, its inspiration, its raison d'être, just as fresh water is for the moai platforms. The similarities are striking, and they lead us to believe that the Europeans had nothing to do with the creation of the local script. That they couldn't possibly have contributed. Meaning that Rongorongo would be the fruit of an autonomous, independent, *free* effort. A language written with no outside interference. An invention. And one whose origins are not so inexplicable, since its trajectory resembles that of other scripts formed under analogous circumstances in very different locations.

In Rapa Nui as in Crete, as in other cases where scripts have been invented, the culture's artistic heritage forms a substratum, a foundation for a wide variety of creative impulses. Art acts as a springboard for writing, a catalyst, a life source, meanwhile endowing it with its graphic structure. Its contribution therefore comes from within, is inherent in its form and logic. From drawing to sign, with no intrusion from outsiders who couldn't possibly understand the originating art or the resulting script.

But why birds? Why riddle the island and their written

language with birds? Why set them, like precious and eternal gems, in the moai's backs? Literally "petrified"—rendered human by art, but also immobile. Why rob them of motion? Because birds could fly away. They could escape the island and return as they pleased. An impossible feat for the islanders of Rapa Nui, forever trapped on their desolate triangle of volcanoes. Alive, but practically extinct.

TANTALUS

The undeciphered scripts of the Aegean—Cretan Hieroglyphic, Linear A, and Cypro-Minoan—may well be hiding completely unknown languages, languages we don't even know exist. That would be a true shame, since the path to reconstructing an unknown language is much more arduous, and the decipherment can never be definitive. There'd be no way to test its validity. If the language were unknown, we'd be stuck in a kind of linguistic limbo, halfway there, our necks twisted, forced always to look behind us, mute, like the diviners in Dante's hell who wanted to *veder troppo davante* (see too far ahead!).

To be stuck midway, looking back, would not be fun: it would mean that we could read the script in question, whichever it may be, by applying phonetic values to the signs, eventually reaching a complete correspondence between sign and sound. But it would also mean that we'd have to stop right there, forever locked outside the gates of understanding the language's morphology. We would never discover how the language functions or to which family it belongs. We would become a new kind of Tantalus, trapped in a pool of water, a fruit tree above us; the water receding as we try to drink, the low-hanging fruit just beyond our reach.

With Rongorongo, it's a different kind of torture, perhaps even more sadistic. The language recorded belongs without doubt to the Polynesian family, and is connected to the modern Rapa Nui language. Back at the turn of the last century, experiments were conducted with the local inhabitants in which they were asked to read various texts. But the results made little sense, except with signs that had a clear natural referent—the sun, a bird, a mouth (though even I could have gotten that far). This of course led to a "pictographic" reading, and to the belief that Rongorongo is a mnemonic system, and therefore unstructured. And that's where the problems begin. It now remains for us to uncover the logical connection between the Rapa Nui language and the structure of its signs. The terms of the equation have been reversed: we know the language, but the typology of the script remains (though not for long, we hope) a complete mystery.

These two elements, script and language, seem to run along parallel tracks. With Rongorongo, it's as if we have a photograph of the finished puzzle (the language), but we can't figure out how to connect all the puzzle pieces (the signs). We can watch the whole film, but we can't thread the scenes back together in sequential order. Or to be more accurate, we can't even put our finger on the film's plot, and the photo of the puzzle is faded, generic, unrelated to the pieces scattered before us.

Understanding the structure, a writing system's typology, is already an important leg up. The next steps are very clear: starting from the logo-syllabary, we must reduce the number of signs in the inventory, and reconstruct the functions of the smaller pieces, the logograms, syllabograms, determinatives.* Figuring out how the pawns move on the linguistic chessboard is the only true way forward. And we're charging ahead with confidence. Just the other day, standing before the three-dimensional image of the Mamari tablet made in Father Alberto's tiny museum—and going teary-eyed just like our geodesists—we noticed several undeniable patterns in the Rongorongo text, from which a clear and identifiable kind of rebus began to emerge. When I suggested, with a measure of caution, "Well, now we can decipher it," one of my researchers replied, in a firm, Obamaish tone of voice I'd never heard him use before, "Oh yes, we can." Technology, a paleographic eye, teamwork, and a bit of logic—I wouldn't be surprised if another small miracle awaits us in the not-so-distant future. One day you find a dodo's egg and, who knows, next thing we're freeing Tantalus from his torture and Dante's diviners from their eternal *contrappasso*.

REBUS

But let's talk for a minute about that "kind of rebus," since the rebus stands as one of the fundamental mechanisms in a script's invention. Let's examine how. Do you recall our friend the syllable? The syllable is essential because syllables are what help produce homophony. The more monosyllabic words there are in a language, the more easily and

---

* A determinative is a sign that marks a word's semantic category, used to help avoid ambiguities in interpretation. For example, in Egyptian hieroglyphs, a determinative will let you know up front that you're speaking of divinities, or parts of the body, or plants, or animals, etc.

instinctively we land on homophony. This homophony is something we're all familiar with. And, in technical terms, it's called a rebus—a tool we're constantly making use of, often without even knowing it.

The name itself is notable, since it comes from the Latin for "thing" (*res*), here in the ablative-instrumental case ("with things"), which brings us around again to the pragmatic concreteness of writing. In the early stages of writing's development, in fact, the rebus was based on logograms, signs that represent things. The crucial point is that a logogram's sound can carry an additional meaning, beyond the one indicated by the drawing. In Old Chinese, the logogram of a horse, pronounced *ma*, is the same *ma* sound that means mother. A logogram can mean two different things, while the sound stays the same. Using this one, small, versatile unit of meaning, we can express two things on completely different ends of the semantic spectrum, and create humor.

To better explain this, we can look to a more modern creation—a highly pictographic form of writing that functions, at least on a base level, just like scripts invented from scratch: emojis.

(And to anyone who groans with disapproval and asks, "What, so you think that with emojis we're going back to hieroglyphs?"—I urge you to respond with a resounding yes! And I'll explain why at the end of this book.)

Are you ready to have some fun? Or do you find emojis to be a ?

There we have it—the rebus. Therein lies the spark, the spell, the beginning of everything. All scripts invented from scratch (even if Mayan is a bit more complicated to reconstruct) make use of rebuses that employ already existent signs, logograms, and expand their semantic value, even to represent concepts that aren't easily communicated at a logographic level. Sumerians, early on, used the sign meaning arrow (*ti*) to represent a beautiful but abstract word, *til*—"life."

Can you 🐝 🍁 it?

Well, you should "bee" "leaf" it—because in English, I'm happy to report, there's a plentitude of homophonic words (whether monosyllabic or disyllabic). I don't have to rack my brain to find great examples in the same vein of "bee" "leaf," which is a composite rebus—wherein two different monosyllabic words produce a third word of a completely different meaning. You don't need to be a genius to find the perfect rebus in English, 🐝 🍁 it 🛶 ⊘ .

In fact, the English language lends itself so well to the principle of the rebus, you can find homophony even within the boundaries of words. ☀️ of a 🔔 ! If this sounds like an obscure concept, don't worry, it's harder to explain than it is to understand. The rebus is instinctive, not intellectual, more intuitive than it is heady. Unravel this one and you'll understand everything.

2 🐝, 🛶 ⊘ 2 🐝.*

A rebus is an instant trick, a miniature revelation. It doesn't take millennia to gestate. One can only imagine how many times, throughout the course of history, someone has realized that one sound can mean two different things. But to put it down in writing—that's something else, something more, since to do so is to set an irreversible process in motion. It's a tantalizing discovery that marks a beginning, that opens the gates—a tiny, clever device that paves the way to real invention.

---

* To be, or not to be.

And I say "discovery" for a reason. Because the way the rebus was used in early writing systems, back at the beginning, helps us to grasp something important: that writing is first and foremost a discovery—a lightbulb of assonance flicking on, a natural turn of phrase, a spontaneous game of expanding the limits of meaning. An intuition—of finding ways to represent words that defy representation with iconic signs. And, in the process, sometimes stumbling on a little humor, which we understand immediately, without lengthy explanations. An invention is something else entirely.

ngae bo wa

pae fo chuu

INVENTED
SCRIPTS

sae kuu sho

choa shu koe

so taa mu

i wo yoe

ri u

Cities

Let's circle back to our two overarching stories and introduce the second. The first story dealt with islands, creation, the fate of undeciphered scripts, with all their mysteries and dark corners. And we'll revisit them later, when they serve as our guinea pigs in the deciphering laboratory. For now, let's talk about success stories, stories of growth and expansion. Let's talk about states and cities, scripts that we can read (with a few exceptions) and languages that we understand. Let's talk about real inventions.

According to current anthropological models, a state and its writing system are always considered to be interdependent, one a function of the other, like the chicken and the egg (even if we don't know which comes first), twin forces in the upward drive toward civilization. The prevailing (and adamantly held) view is that complex society—which culminates in the state (or the city, understood as a micro-state)—cannot *not* develop an equally complex writing system. Following this logic, we'd have to say that a city can't function without a writing system, and a writing system without a city is doomed inexorably to die. Which would make the city and writing an indissoluble binomial that demonstrates just how articulate, complex, skilled, and cognitively "advanced" human beings are. Right? All clear?

Except this model doesn't work. It's true that the great

cultures of antiquity—Egypt, Mesopotamia, Mesoamerica, China—all sooner or later invented a script. And all, it seems, in an independent and autonomous way, without external input. Four flashes of genius, four inventions (we're almost certain). But this doesn't mean that writing is an essential factor in determining a culture's complexity. Quite the opposite. As we'll see, the world is teeming with magnificent cultures that never produced a writing system, and, alternatively, writing systems that took root in the fertile loam of society and came bursting up unexpectedly, green and vibrant, right through the middle of a strip of asphalt. The felicitous results of who knows what kind of creative-alchemical combinations, sprouting in the most unlikely of places.

It always pays to proceed cautiously with models and categories—all it takes is one faulty link, one exception, one unique case, and the logical chain is broken. In the words of the physicist Richard Feynman, the exception proves that the rule is wrong. But that hasn't stopped us from organizing the world into neatly defined categories by taxonomizing life (what have you done to us, Aristotle?). Symmetry and order create a sense of control, of peace. We humans feel less like animals when we use our rationality to systematize, to tidy up our surroundings, creating a false sense of security, slapping a Band-Aid over the unpredictable. It's tough, isn't it, embracing true beauty, the beauty of chaos? And it's even tougher to sit back, hands folded, and resist our obsessive impulse to organize.

Which is all to say that a state/city and its relationship to its writing system must not only be correlated but measured in reciprocal relation to all of the other factors that, very clearly, play a role in defining a culture's complexity (trade, urbanization, social stratification, skill specialization, subsistence economy, and our old pal writing, of course). The question is: Are there universal patterns, certain ingredients that are essential to cultural evolution? To get to *x*, do we first have to go through *a-b-c-d*, etc.? And are we capable of measuring all this, of making a list of essential ingredients, *conditiones sine qua non*?

There are two types of people in the world: those who make lists (to-do lists, to-not-do lists, shopping lists, bucket lists) and those who don't. From what I can tell, we list-makers are a robust crew (there's a notebook on my desk with OBSESSIVE LISTS written in gold lettering across the cover). I, it goes without saying, belong to the category of hard-core list-o-holics, perhaps not in the top percentile, but somewhere up there. It would seem that a third of list-o-holics write their lists in code, using acronyms that make no sense to anyone else (I'm one of them, naturally). True list-o-holics write exclusively by hand—making lists on the computer is like studying on Wikipedia: nothing sticks. It's all gone by the morning. Plus, what about that triumphant satisfaction you feel when you press your pen to the page and cross out an item with a nice fat line? Wiped from the list. Completed. And there's nothing like reading back over a list of crossed-out items to set the universe straight. Even just writing about it now I feel a little better.

Though it must be said: lists do make us feel good, but it's only a placebo effect. And they don't always work. So, are cities and writing on the list of ingredients that make up a complex society? Let's find out.

BUREAUMANIA

Many too many are born: the state was invented
for the superfluous! Just see how it lures them, the

> many-too-many! How it devours them, and chews
> them, and rechews them! There is nothing greater
> on earth than I, the regulating finger of God.
> —Friedrich Nietzsche, *Thus Spoke Zarathustra*

A little anthropology lesson. Social complexity has three levels of development. The most advanced is the state, followed by egalitarian society and then stratified society under the rule of a leader (a "chiefdom"). The earliest states, the most ancient, took shape on their own, with no other similar entities there to influence them. They developed by accumulating layers of complexity, by slowly acquiring the ingredients on the list of items necessary for their growth. And if they're the most ancient, that means they're at the very root of statehood—the primitive egg to the complex chicken of society. Their development is therefore original, pristine. We call them "primary" states. From zero to state, with no one butting their nose in.

A primary state does develop in contact with others— trade enlivens a state and helps it grow—but its foundation is authentic; it happens in one place and nowhere else; it germinates, grows, stratifies, and expands. It has a well-defined center that controls the rest of the territory. Centralization brings with it strategies and norms for exercising that control. The more territory a state covers, the more forcefully must the center exert its power. When human beings expand, we tend to create some pretty perverse things, such as bureaucracy. To maintain control, the central authority invests itself with rules—it *bureaucratizes* (truly, the word may be even uglier than the thing itself). The birth of bureaucracy is thus tied to the birth of the state.

We can get a closer look at primary state formations

through archaeological evidence found in Mesoamerica, in the Oaxaca Valley and at the site of Monte Albán, where bureaucratized institutional buildings and temples were constructed around 300–100 BCE (the same years as Rome's expansion, more or less). In the early centuries of the first millennium CE, we see a similar expansion in Peru, on the northern coast (Gallinazo culture). Much earlier, around the midpoint of the fourth millennium BCE, Egypt (the Naqada period, I and II) and Mesopotamia (in Uruk, modern-day Iraq) were developing neck and neck, expanding their territories, constructing palaces and centers of power. A few centuries later (3200–2600 BCE), the same phenomenon occurred in the Indus Valley, with the birth of the Harappa culture; and in central China, not long after (1800–1500 BCE), at Erlitou, in the Henan region, along the Yellow River.

Six cradles across the globe, each the fruit of an independent cultural tradition. Six nuclei of complexity, six bureaucratic hubs. Bureaucracy, however, doesn't function as a system of oral commands communicated over wireless phones. It depends upon a network of delegates and the broad transmission of information—it depends upon the concreteness of messages. Which is why the birth of bureaucracy means, in the end, the birth of writing.

The ingredients on the "complexity list" are often interconnected. We can now say, with near scientific certainty, that wherever there's a state with a population of more than ten thousand, you can bet there's a writing system. One appears just as the other is rearing its head. We're not sure which comes first, but the catalysis is reciprocal. Both seem to be phenomena brought about by the forces of environmental selection (demographic growth, agricultural production, storage of goods, etc.), just like punctuated events in Darwinian evolutionary development (the term *punctu-ated*, in fact, is taken wholesale from biology and here applied to anthropology).

A domino falls, a fuse is lit, a perfect storm of factors brings about a change. There's no keeping track of evolution's inner workings—it's a machine that speeds up and slows down as it pleases, but it never stops. Between these periods of evolutionary upheaval (the birth of primary states and the birth of writing, in our case) come long periods of stability, during which everything remains more or less the same, in a reassuring homeostatic equilibrium. God rested on the seventh day because, in the turn of a week, he'd brought about a real revolution. (And there was writing. And it was good.)

AN IMPERFECT MATCH

Though of course, that's not the case. Empires, civilizations, cultures have existed without a writing system, and writing systems have formed like pearls in oysters, with no warning, no territorial expansion, no clear purpose. And if we remove its bureaucratic function from the equation, the role of writing seems to lose its value. So how do we frame it, then?

There are indeed certain factors that favor the invention of writing, but they aren't all necessarily connected to rampant bureaucracy. Writing's birth involves elements of chance, aspects that lists and models and rigged equations can't categorize or explain. Some marriages work even when friends and relatives are placing bets at the ceremony on when (and not if) the couple will get a divorce. It's the same with scripts—some scripts, anyway. All of a sudden they're celebrating their fiftieth anniversary, against all the odds. Or else they're like nags at the racetrack, leaving thoroughbreds in their dust. Let's take a look at them, why don't we, these underdog champions, these quixotic Rocinantes. There's one thing that's clear, at least: they're far more interesting than a boring bureaucratic list.

Archaeological and ethnographic data can help us paint a clearer picture of just how writing systems formed in unexpected places (unexpected, at least, if we're following outdated models).* Right off the bat it's clear that scripts flourished outside the institution of the bureaucratized state, that they were vibrant and, above all, highly creative. I'll cite only a few examples, each brimming with insights.

We'll start with the runes. In the Norse saga *Edda*, with its king-sorcerer Odin, the runes are the magical inscriptions carved into the tree of life, Yggdrasil, by the Norns, beings who spin the thread of man's fate. (I first encountered these tales in elementary school, and the idea that their script was "secret" made me wild with joy.) The alphabet, in technical terms, goes by the name of Futhark, and is very clearly adapted from the Roman alphabet, with a few Etruscan touches. Evidence of it can be found on thousands of objects engraved in Denmark and northern Germany during the second century CE (fig. 10). Spells, divinations, fortunes, predictions—the full panoply of magic. And no central government to speak of.

Then there's Tifinagh, an ancient consonantal script (like Arabic), which is still used today to record the Berber Tuareg languages in North Africa. These populations were most certainly not structured at the state level, nor did they

* My thanks to Alex de Voogt, whose ethnographic studies were of great help to me in writing this section.

10. An inscription in Futhark, in Ärentuna, Sweden

develop a specialized governing class. Not only is Tifinagh beautiful, it seems to be no more than vaguely influenced by Phoenician, in the shape of its signs. One other unique, and therefore fascinating, aspect is that the Tuaregs belong to a society where communication is principally oral, based largely on memory. Writing, there, does not carry the same function that it does in other cultures. It seems to have been invented for fun, for puzzle-making, for the occasional inscription or graffiti. Just take a closer look: it's like something out of a science-fiction film. Beautiful, simple, and free of any strict purpose (fig. 11).

11. An inscription in Tifinagh, in Algeria

On the African continent there are at least fourteen sub-Saharan scripts, created by groups that wanted their own writing system, even before launching independence movements. And then there's China, where, in the southwest region at the foot of the Himalayas, the Nakhi are an ethnic minority—and a small one at that, compared with their Tibetan neighbors to the north. Yet, a thousand years ago, the Nakhi created something miraculous with which to inscribe their religious texts: a highly iconic, logo-syllabic writing system, Dongba. If you visit Lijiang, in Yunnan Province, you can see it in action, since Dongba is in the midst of a fascinating revival. You'll find it on shop signs and street signs, even though almost no one knows how to read or write it. It carries a social and political value. It's a manifesto, a means of expressing their Nakhi (and not Chinese) identity. Look how they've altered a modern Starbucks sign (fig. 12)—which bears no fewer than three scripts: Dongba,

12. A Starbucks sign in Dongba (Nakhi), China

in small lettering, up at the top, followed by Chinese, and then the roman alphabet. In the Dongba text, the first sign is three stars (*star*), the second sign a flower (or *bbaq*), and the third sign a dog (*kee*). Even an American coffee shop can take on a Nakhi flavor.

Then there are the Caroline Islands in Micronesia, in the Pacific, where the local populations, beginning in the 1900s, invented a syllabary to record their language, Woleaian. It was not, alas, destined to survive. But if we look carefully at the script (fig. 13), we find incredibly inventive elements—not least its reworking of the Latin alphabet, on which its signs are based, and a series of completely new signs, invented from scratch, whose syllables were developed on the basis of . . . you guessed it . . . a rebus. The syllable *pu*, which in Woleaian means "fish," was shaped like a fish, *shrü* was shaped like a fishbone, *lö* like a bottle, *ngä* like bamboo, *warr* a canoe. And that's precisely what the Carolinian signs were used for, to decorate your canoe or the walls of your home, not to collect taxes. The sea, the ocean, was their master, not the state. We should also mention the Cherokee and the Cree syllabaries, and the Inuktitut scripts in the northern United States and Canada. No central government, just peoples and their languages.

On the flip side, we have Kerma, an ancient culture from the Sudan region, which formed a state nearly five thousand years ago. Kerma culture dominated Upper Nubia for at least a thousand years, along the banks of the Nile. The Egyptians referred to it as Kush. The people of Kush were no cowards—they were valiant warriors, skilled archers. They traded in ivory, gold, ebony. And their writing system? Never happened.

The list could go on. States and scripts make for an imperfect match, an arranged marriage, a dubious pair.

13. The syllabary of the Caroline Islands (Woleai)

The most grievous error, however, is to label bureaucracy as the ultimate aim—the beginning and end—of writing. This is just reckless drivel, which for far too long has cast its shadow over the greatest invention in the world, stripping it of its soul (as all misguided generalizations do). The heart of writing beats in the brain and in human language, in the imagination, in our need to anchor ourselves to the earth that sustains us, in our deep desire to name—ourselves, and everything around us. Not in the oval office of the bloodless monster that is the state, purveyor of taxes, tickets, and lists of expenditures.

INVENTION, INTENTION

What is an invention, exactly? "The creation of something that didn't exist before," you're probably thinking. And you're right. Put in those terms, invention is tied to the awareness of an absence, which it then fills by creating something from nothing. You detect a problem and then find a way to solve it. As was the case with the first tools, especially Neolithic tools: whether to chip or break or cut something, they formed sharp and hard (flint) instruments fit for the task. Think about the (similar) problem of bringing food to our mouths: by ingeniously adding a handle to a spoon, we refined (with a better grip) an activity we'd already partly sorted out (scooping). Same with the fork, for skewering and for twirling our spaghetti. You might say your hands are more efficient, but not when it comes to piercing solids and ladling liquids. We need the tool to solve the problem.

If to invent, therefore, is to find a remedy, then the bureaucrats were right: writing was invented to fulfill the

need of managing land and people. I can't remember who it was who said that the pen is mightier than the sword.*
But if that were really the case, then we'd have to consider the invention of writing to be intentional, a planned and systematic effort. No accident along the way, no intuitive flash: a deliberate act. And a conscious act, at that, done with cognitive awareness.

Which means that we have a problem. Or at least I do, since the title of this book is *The Greatest Invention*, and here I am about to double down on my claim that writing was sparked by a flash of insight and is not, at least at its origins, an invention. And I'd go even further. For me, invention equals intention, but when it comes to understanding writing, thinking in terms of necessity and clear objectives is of little use. The idea of necessity (that is, the urgency of finding a solution to a problem) is not always at the root of invention. In fact, the opposite is often true—we discover a thing first, only to later find that it has a practical application, perhaps far different than what we'd initially imagined. Do you recall the rebus, and the way the homophony lightbulb went off in our heads? *That* is an example of discovery. Invention comes later, as an effect of discovery. And it is piecemeal, gradual, magnificently layered. It needs to be broken in—it needs time, and energy, before it becomes intention.

The moment has arrived to take a tour of the true inventions in writing's history—those built from the ground up, completely original, influenced by no other culture that may

* I checked: the quote is officially attributed to Edward Bulwer-Lytton, a politician and writer (so he knew what he was talking about), but the phrase is as old as the hills and I have no doubt that someone thought of it before him.

have developed something similar. We'll explore inventions in Egypt, China, Mesopotamia, and Mesoamerica, and how they adhered to a model only up to a certain point—that is, as long as that model allowed for adaptability, flexibility, and regard for the ever-changing conditions of life.

The greatest inventions in history—from the wheel to electricity, from computers to nuclear fission—are all born, without exception, from the spark of discovery. In that millisecond of creative and vital intuition—voilà—entire revolutions take place. Refining these revolutionary discoveries, making them whole, is what invention truly is: the complete process, the full circle. This requires dedication, time, intuition, foresight, and planning.

So let's zoom in now on the gears and cogs of this ingenious, human, and imperfect mechanism. Let's have a look at this great invention.

THE FOREST

One hundred years ago, the economist Frank Knight formalized a distinction between uncertainty and risk. Uncertainty, he said, is the absence of knowledge, and is therefore impossible to calculate. Risk, on the other hand, is measurable, since it can be calculated using a probability distribution of potential results or outcomes. With uncertainty there's little you can do—ontologically speaking, *you cannot be certain about uncertainty.* Yet, by definition, both uncertainty and risk are ways of projecting the future.

Engaged, as we are, with the invention of writing, our realm is the realm of the past. And when you're dealing with the past, every method of verification has its holes.

We're always at risk of getting it wrong. Which is why we've been wrestling for so many years—and still are, in part—with one of the most important questions: How many times has writing been invented? How can we determine this with any degree of probability, if not certainty?

Up until about forty years ago, we were convinced that writing had been invented only once in all of human history. So widespread was this conviction that it was baptized with a pompous name, resounding in its staunch creationism: monogenesis. One invention, end of story, no other explanations accepted. Nothing is ever invented twice—as you know, man can't reinvent the wheel, and therefore, in conclusion, etc., etc.

If you take a leap back into your own past, I'm sure this authoritarian version of events will sound familiar—a vague, Proustian memory will come wafting over you, from your days in elementary or middle school, something about Mesopotamia and how cuneiform was the first and only time writing was invented, the source from which all other scripts descend. As we know, however, the neurons in our hippocampus toy with our memories and compromise their clarity. So it may be that you've completely forgotten what your beloved teacher said just after that: "However, we have still yet to determine the exact number of times that this invention has occurred." (I, too, like the hippocampus, am prone to tweaking your memories, since your teacher probably never said anything of the sort.)

Over the last forty years, since the time I was born, things have shifted substantially, and the view that writing was invented only once is no longer so categorical. The inscriptions from Mesoamerica, which we've been deciphering gradually from the 1970s on, are clear evidence of a true invention, free of outside influence—even if it was only through gritted teeth that the "monogenesists" accepted the theory that Mayan glyphs constitute a veritable writing system. How could these Native American symbols, so heterogeneous, so fantastical, ever be compared with the thin and perfect wedges of Mesopotamia, the true cradle of civilization?

In science as in life, if you find at least two clear-cut cases, you should probably start looking for others. Egypt's earliest writings are not only close to being contemporary with Mesopotamia's (the beginning of the fourth millennium BCE), they may have even come first, from what we can tell. For which reason it's likely that Egypt, too, created its writing system from scratch, autonomously, with no external interference, perhaps even before cuneiform. And China—if somewhat later, toward the end of the second millennium BCE—invented a completely new system, utterly different from the Egyptian and Mesopotamian scripts.

Four inventions, now all but proven. Though could there be others, still? We have no definitive answer, but it's likely that there are. And we've already mentioned them. Easter Island may have created Rongorongo on its own, uninfluenced by European colonizers. And the Indus Valley developed the highly repetitive and formulaic Harappa "script." Though there's still much disagreement around this latter case, since its status as a full-fledged writing system is up for debate.

To answer the question "How many times?" one must keep the larger picture in mind, without losing sight of the various local contexts and details. Inventing a script involves certain necessary steps, which, as we'll see, come with their own structural restrictions and present a number of commonalities, whether the invention is created ex nihilo or not. Inventions, in other words, travel along separate but parallel tracks, following similar paths to formation. These paths resemble one another at the foundational and structural level, which does nothing to subtract from the splendor of their differences. It's therefore not only *possible* that writing has been invented many times throughout human history, it's also highly *probable*.

Taking a global view means accounting for both aspects: similarities and differences. Those of us who study writing systems (though perhaps not only us) must move beyond a local, isolated, restricted view of things, steering well clear of our current obsession with specialization. We must move beyond the Aegean, Egypt, Mesopotamia, and China, and embrace the entire expanse of the world. Without borders. It's well past time we stop acting like people who've seen thousands of trees but have never truly seen the forest.

Before the Pharaohs

Egypt is an unusual place. In an ancient world where few knew how to read or write, and so little has survived of the little that was written, Egypt gifted us with rivers of words, and not a single one out of place or redundant. In its graphomania, Egypt sets us swirling in an eddy of images, narratives, portraits of great men, tales of the dead who went toe-to-toe with eternity. To give you a sense of the breadth and intensity of this "Nile" of words, here's a literary comparison: if writing itself were a writer, Egyptian hieroglyphs would be Leo Tolstoy, who wrote without pause, no matter when, where, or how small the detail. Tolstoy was a graphomaniac, and so was Egypt four thousand years before him. And just as Tolstoy brought his characters to life, the Egyptians did the same with their writing. Egyptian signs are infused with a vital spirit: to erase a written name was to murder that person; to scratch out the sign of a dangerous animal was to render it harmless. But here we're talking about Egypt at its pharaonic height. The early days were different.

All beginnings, in truth, are arbitrary, often mysterious, and sometimes accidental. It's difficult, if not impossible, to point out the precise moment in a process that marks its beginning. And so, unlike Tolstoy, and unlike Egypt in its later years, the invention of writing in Egypt is a laconic affair, almost stenographic. The first hieroglyphs, strangely enough, bring to mind one of the great Tolstoyan protagonists, so expertly drawn in his reflective and laconic nature as to seem a portrait of the author himself: naturally, a human being who writes much can't help but be a human being who speaks little. With just one scene from a novel, we can understand the first hieroglyphic inscriptions: when Levin asks Kitty to marry him for the second time.* Levin writes his marriage proposal in code, scribbling on the table with a piece of chalk. He uses only the first letter of each word (*w y t m i c n b d t m n o t*). She understands instantly (a skillful decipherer, that Kitty)† and accepts, replying in the same way, initial by initial.

Sometimes (and only sometimes) it takes so little to understand each other.

The earliest hieroglyphs are not all that different from Levin's marriage proposal to Kitty. We're on a hot and arid desert plain, not far from the Nile. It's 1988, and a German archaeologist and his team discover an enormous tomb (Tomb U-j), composed of twelve interconnected rooms. The impressive tomb is located in an equally impressive cemetery, although architecturally speaking it's the most elaborate, prominently positioned at the center—preeminent. We're in the vicinity of Abydos, and the necropolis goes by the name of Umm El Qa'āb, "mother of pots," after all the ceramic pot shards littering the area.

* On his first attempt, she refuses him because she's waiting for a proposal from another man—the novel's villain, naturally.
† I'll give you a hand: "When you told me it could never be, did that mean never, or then?"

Centuries later, not far from here, the Egyptians will construct the temple of the pharaoh Seti I, father of Ramesses II. But in this moment, 3,320 years before Christ, there's still no trace of pharaohs. Keep this date in mind, 3,320 years before Christ, more than 5,000 years ago. We're still in Predynastic Egypt, and in the tombs at Abydos we find abundant evidence of something else, something far more important: a first (though still debated) attempt at writing.

These earliest symbols appear on pottery, seal impressions, and some three hundred ivory tags the size of stamps (fig. 14), with a hole in the corner so that they could be strung to various goods, such as textiles, leather pouches, or pots. The signs found on these labels are reminiscent (to a certain degree) of the Egyptian hieroglyphs that we'll find in droves in later periods. And it's these signs that interest us in particular.

Also of interest are several important pottery vessels from the East, with traces of resinated wine and figs, sealed shut using impressed seals. Predynastic Egyptians drank sweet wine, wine of a certified quality, sealed to guarantee its authenticity. Not so different from the modern labels we find on bottles of wine or any other product we're trying to market. The seal represents the brand, and to launch it, all you need are a few words and an image. Think about the logos everywhere around us today. It's precisely the same.

These artifacts are buried with the dead and for the dead, to uphold their memory: they seem to speak to us of who they are, to tell of their affairs. Among them may indeed be the king of Upper Egypt, Scorpion I, his arachnid emblem engraved repeatedly around him, to celebrate his legacy as king. These labels are the ancient equivalent of keywords in modern marketing: an expression of quality,

14. Labels inscribed in Ancient Egyptian,
Tomb U-j at Abydos

authenticity, ownership. At Abydos we find the prehistory of the brand, and, perhaps, the true beginning of writing's invention.

THE GRAMMAR OF CREATION

Though the ivory tags found at Tomb U-j in Abydos bear only a few sparse symbols and brief sign sequences, the tags themselves are numerous. The engraved signs depict the forms of animals, plants, men, and mountains, as well as linear and geometric symbols. Among the various categories attested, some are linked to the celebration of power, be it divine or temporal, and to the quantity and variety of the material goods recorded. Some signs seem to form a kind of narrative—there's even suggestion of a human sacrifice. These representations are unusual, since even though some symbols do resemble the hieroglyphs found in later periods, the same can't be said about all the rest, which are without parallel. How are we supposed to read them? And then, as we know, labels weren't the only type of engraved object. We find more than a hundred inscriptions on pottery, painted with ink, using signs such as scorpions, fish, falcons, and boats.

Are we here in the presence of a full-fledged script? Is this where the invention truly begins? The debate, of course, is ongoing, and the stakes are extremely high. Here's why. If the inscriptions found at Tomb U-j represent a fully formed script, then we're going to have to overhaul our traditional view of how writing was invented—a view that's been gospel for years, taught in schools, passed down from generation to generation. Mesopotamia would have to be knocked down a peg—no longer number one, no longer first in the invention of writing. A new order would have to be established.

I relish these debates, especially when the underdog topples the favorite by just a few points. So let's get down into the details. The material isn't easy to interpret, and it's limited (though not scanty). But the system of symbols seems to possess its own logic and coherence.

Mixed among the figures of humans, reptiles, and mammals is one other sign that will enjoy a long life, the *serekh*, depicting the niched façade of a palace, topped by a falcon.

This sign is a heraldic emblem that always represents the king. The combinations of these signs on the tags vary—a trait that's indicative of a writing system, not just a simple set of drawings. It's as if the Predynastic Egyptians buried in this tomb adopted their preexisting iconography for another purpose, to represent something else: combinations of sound. Highly recognizable, iconic symbols, emblems, rearranged with linguistic dexterity. Or at least that's how it seems.

There are those, on the other hand, who maintain that the similarities between these signs and the later script are extremely limited: just a few birds, some water, maybe a cobra. A few uniconsonantal sounds, in other words, only coincidentally related to the "classical" hieroglyphs. A random, icon-based system, with a loose connection at best to the later symbols. An inspiration, in short, the groundwork, but not a script. It lacks the sufficient level of form and structure to be one.

There is, however, a method, an order to these ancient tags. They're trying to communicate something precise, something beyond the snapshot of information we get from a drawing. They are charged with words. They speak to us, and not just in any old way, but in Egyptian. Names and designations seem to be recorded using single signs, signs reminiscent of logograms. But that's not all: in some cases, one sign helps us to understand another, lending information about its sound or meaning. Let's look at an example: a combination of the sign for elephant and the sign for mountain, which we'd render with the toponym $ȝbw$, Elephantine. The place indicated by the two signs is not Elephant ($ȝbw$) + Mountain ($ḥȝs.t$), but the city of Elephantine ($ȝbw$). In other words, we're already in the early stages of the rebus:

the mountain sign tells us that we're dealing with a top-onym, a place name, and not just an animal. The sound is the same, but the semantic category is different. Rebus.

We find this little trick on other tags, too—and not just toponyms, but names of people, along with other ingredients that aren't quite clear to us but that nonetheless fall into coherent sequences, mixed in with figurative symbols. There's a logic behind them, and it shows. So to say that we're still "behind the curve" of writing is a little ungenerous. And there aren't just signs! There are numbers, too. And these numbers, even though they don't appear together with signs on the labels, but separately on their own labels, still give us an important sense of just how cognitively advanced Predynastic Egyptians were. Numbers, as we'll see in Mesopotamia as well, are the trusty co-pilots in the early race to the first scripts: they pitch in, help steady the craft, guide the way. In Egypt, they were already using a base-ten system—a system that remains in place to this day and that here seems already well articulated.

The seal impressions, meanwhile, make for a rival attraction. They include no signs associated with a script, but are done in the same style as the ivory tags. They follow the same compositional logic and serve as a decorative counterpoint. They're flattering, in other words—the perfect companion piece for the tags and their hieroglyphic-style signs.

All, in short, would seem to indicate that we're in the presence of an early go at written language, hieroglyphs in embryo, just waiting to take flight. Invention, liftoff! Though you know better by now—invention happens in stages. It's a slow process of accumulating the necessary linguistic understanding, of selecting the proper form for each sign. It's a lever effect, one of those simple machines that allow for movement in one direction only. Like the teeth on a gear, turning gradually and steadily. We'll call it the ratchet effect, if we're being technical. And with the ratchet effect, there's no turning back.

ENCROACHMENT

And there's no slowing this machine down—the gears, in fact, only keep turning faster, their teeth moving ceaselessly around and around. In the span of a hundred years, still early in the First Dynasty, writing spreads and is used to complement the iconographic decorations on ceremonial objects, like the famous tablets or votive slabs such as the Narmer Palette (fig. 15). Names, as ever, are the main focus of the inscriptions, along with other related terms that refer to the current rulers. The inventory of hieroglyphs grows and solidifies, becoming a fully formed system in a relatively brief period of time. And all the mechanisms are present, even if longer, more complex syntax doesn't come until later.

The aim of this writing is clear. The Egyptians took great pride in calling out the identities of their rulers, celebrating their prestige with gusto and a profusion of hieroglyphs. And hieroglyphs, given their iconic nature, never come alone: they work in tandem with images, iconographic compositions. These two elements, writing and image, are constantly encroaching on each other's territory, in a powerful "visual" dance. It's as if the hieroglyphic writing acts as an exhibit of monumentality, to celebrate the important names, while the images seem to work to make this intention all the more apparent, in a truly harmonious choreography. What's amazing, and rare, about it all, is that neither

15. The Narmer Palette

of the two elements steals the show: hieroglyph and orna-
mentation lean on and rely on each other, as partners. Finally, a relationship with a little equality.

But this act of encroachment doesn't stop there. It con-
tinues beyond the borders of Egypt. It invades the birth
of writing as a whole. We've already mentioned one other
instance of encroachment: the possibility that Egypt may
have invented writing before Mesopotamia. As I noted, the
jury has yet to issue a final verdict, even though the evidence is stacking up. And if it turns out to be true, it would
mean that Egyptian hieroglyphs preceded cuneiform by

nearly a century—which, when you think about it, is no small matter.

But there's still one other realm that hieroglyphs invade, and it's one of fundamental importance, because it's the realm of causality—the very purpose of writing's existence, from the beginnings of its invention. Mesopotamia, in its role as the presumed first inventor, cast a long shadow over the general reasons for which writing came to be invented. As we'll see, the Mesopotamians, in order to govern their palaces, were forced to keep detailed records of their mechanisms of control. Bureaucracy reigned supreme, a highly complex mechanism even at its very outset. And here again come our bureaumaniacs, clambering in through the windows, after all we'd done to boot them out the door. But let's hold them at bay for just a minute longer.

In an Egypt busy molding itself into a pharaonic kingdom, writing is impertinent. It pokes its head in, to serve as a foil, to call attention to the VIPs. It slips between the cracks of images, forming a syntax of individuals, a pyramid of names. It's obsessed with celebrity. The classic image we have in our heads of the Egyptian bureaucratic state is based on an Egypt that would come into being only much later. And even when writing is employed in service of the state, it nonetheless remains anchored to its underlying ideological framework, as we can see in the self-representations found at tombs from the Old Kingdom.

Celebration. We must rid ourselves of the idea that societies, in order to become the Leviathan that is the state, cannot survive without developing methods of control tied inextricably to the linguistic formalism of writing. Because they can, let's face it—especially when we take the narrow, limited, constricting view of writing as a tool used merely for controlling, not creating, accounting, not celebrating.

THE STONE GUEST

This book, as I've said from the outset, is not a book on the alphabet, the one we all know, the one you're reading right now. I've purposefully avoided it, though I'm aware that it's been hovering around like the Commendatore in Mozart's *Don Giovanni*. The alphabet is uncontainable, pervasive, even more present in its absence. We Westerners—and we're not alone—are so caught up in our alphabetic superiority complex that we've sanctioned its creation as the only valid currency in human communication, the bread at nearly every dinner table. And there's no doubt that its genealogy, its family tree, traces an incredible success story, the rise of a nearly global empire. With few exceptions, all the alphabets in the world—not just the Roman alphabet (our own), but the Greek, Cyrillic, Arabic, Hebrew, and Thai alphabets, too—were cast in the same mold. And that mold is the Egyptian hieroglyphic script.

The alphabet won its place in history because it is revolutionary. Even I have to admit it, and I'm a little biased, but the evidence is clear. It has a limited number of signs in its repertoire, each letter corresponds to a sound (known also as a segmental system), it's relatively easy to learn, it's convenient, flexible, comfortable. It is, without question, the Occam's razor of scripts. The Maserati of writing systems.

Though it's also true that history takes its liberties—it doesn't always follow a clear and linear path toward simplicity. The course of history is filled with crossroads, with paths that fork at random, with potholes, curves, and, yes, accidents. That we eventually arrived at the alphabet may well be because we missed another turn along the way, because we blew past an intersection, because other cars traveling just as fast were thwarted by a pothole. We arrived at the alphabet, to the detriment of all the numerous other forms that writing has taken throughout history—the variations and modulations and adaptations. And so far it's worked out for us. But the winner isn't always the one who deserved it most. The alphabet won, yes, but you'd never have predicted it based on its beginnings.

We're in the desert of the Sinai Peninsula, 1900 BCE, nearly four thousand years ago, though the date may have been a century or two later. It's not the most hospitable of places: the Egyptians have installed an outpost there, a mine for extracting turquoise, along with a temple dedicated to the goddess of turquoise (and of miners), Hathor. Hathor protects all. Even the workers who came from the Nile Delta, and who spoke no Egyptian, only a Northwest Semitic dialect (called Canaanite). We know this because of inscriptions—some forty of them, carved into rock or small objects like statuettes—found along the path that led to the temple. The inscriptions make use of Egyptian hieroglyphs, though not to record the Egyptian language. They record the Canaanite dialect. In short, the hieroglyphic signs were adopted for a different language, repurposed to represent that language's sounds. The hieroglyph depicting the head of an ox, for example, is given the Canaanite name ʾalp ("ox"); the hieroglyph depicting a house takes the Canaanite name bayt ("house"); the hieroglyph depicting a stick is given the Canaanite name giml ("stick"), and so on.

An ingenious experiment, carried out on the margins of institutional culture, far from the city, by an unlikely group of half-illiterates intent on celebrating a goddess and increasing the wealth of the Egyptian kingdom. It's almost incredible that the origins of our alphabet (*aleph*, *beyt*, *giml*) could be so humble, so unassuming, so lacking in fanfare.

Though it's true, of course, that little steps make the big steps possible. And it's also true that the Greeks were the alphabet's first real publicists, many centuries later. But this small beginning, this first bud of creation, might have finished in the scrap heap just as naturally and unpredictably as it came into existence. Things could have gone very, very differently. And all it would have taken was one fork in the road. One wrong turn.

SLIDING DOORS

Allow me to tell you a story, to illustrate a point. And forgive me if I warp the plot a little to suit my needs—I hereby grant myself poetic license.

Gwynethpaltrow 1 catches the subway at the last second. When she gets back home, she catches her boyfriend in the act of cheating. She kicks him out of the house, gives herself a chic, '90s-style pixie cut, becomes a successful entrepreneur, and finds the man of her dreams. Gwynethpaltrow 2, however, misses the subway, goes on dating her traitorous boyfriend, does little to nothing with her life until one day she's struck by a bus. I present to you the Gwynethpaltrow 1 and Gwynethpaltrow 2 of the alphabet: Abgad and Halaḥam. Both are derived from Proto-Sinaitic, both are attested at least five centuries later, and the alphabet both use is formally the same. The only difference is the order of their letters.

To explain: there exist tablets that bear the abecedarium—the sequence of letters—in the proper order. These tablets were a learning tool, for teaching students how to read and write the letters of the alphabet. They functioned as a literacy textbook. The abecedarium presented two letter sequences: one, called Abgad, followed the North Semitic order (*alep, bet, giml, dalet*), and the other fell in a different sequence, the so-called South Semitiç order, or Halaḥam, a name derived from the sounds of the first four letters (*he, lamed, heth, mem*).

The common link between these two alphabets is a city in Syria called Ugarit. In Ugarit, toward the end of the second millennium BCE, centuries after the rise of the Proto-Sinaitic alphabet, the population spoke a North Semitic dialect, very similar to Phoenician. Schools taught this local language, Ugaritic, using abecedaria inscribed with wedge-like signs, not unlike those used in cuneiform, as we'll see (fig. 16). Their writing style was similar to Mesopotamian,

16. An abecedarium in Ugaritic cuneiform, Ugarit, Syria

but the letters' sounds were local, Semitic. And it was in Ugarit that these two different alphabetical orders, Abgad and Halaḥam, came together—coexisting, if only briefly, in the same schools.

But a gust of wind, a twist of fate, an unexpected fork soon sets them on different paths and destinies. Abgad is taken up by Phoenician merchants. It becomes a successful entrepreneur, hawking its economical, practical, and highly efficient product. It opens franchises all across the world, is adopted by the Greeks, and learns to speak hundreds of languages over the centuries. It becomes Mr. Alphabet.

Halaḥam departs from Ugarit, heading south, and is trampled beneath the caravans of the Arabian Peninsula, lost between the desert dunes—the only trace left of it a few measly headstones, engraved with sparse inscriptions. Beautiful, but provincial, peripheral. Soon to be the pet project of bookworms and bespectacled professors whose hearts race whenever they see a rare inscription (me). Halaḥam is destined for oblivion, despite itself. Halaḥam is a victim of chance: one bad throw of the dice. Which brings us to our stone guest, who yells at Don Giovanni: "Repent!" But Don Giovanni repents nothing. And he dies all the same.

Between Two Rivers

TOKENISM

It's said that in Mesopotamia, the region between the Tigris and the Euphrates in modern-day Iraq, writing was born from pebbles—thousands of ancient pebbles, spread across the entire Middle East, an immense area. From Pakistan to Iraq, to Iran, and into parts of what is now Turkey. The earliest pebbles date back to more than ten thousand years ago, when the traces left by man were still vagrant, like footprints in the sand, and settlements were rare.

The history of these pebbles is as long as the history of man's first civilizations, the discovery of agriculture, the moment when people stopped moving and started planting trees. The earliest inklings of Mesopotamian writing are intimately tied to the earth, to the primal idea of house and home. The script that took rise in Mesopotamia is a durable, solid, ordered script, even in its developing phases. Its stability is the stability of settling down, throwing up walls, building a home.

Not everyone accepts this theory that writing was born from pebbles, but it has long held sway, casting its considerable shadow over the origins of writing. Here's what it entails. These pebbles were small stone or clay symbols, technically called "tokens," and were molded into a variety of geometric shapes: spheres, crescents, parallelepipeds, cones. Each shape was used to indicate a different trade good. Before developing a standard format using tablets, goods and objects were counted with tokens: the sheep had its token, cows and bread had theirs, and so on. Nearly five hundred types of tokens in all. Once they'd finished their accounting, they'd shut some of the tokens safely away in a hollow clay sphere. A ball full of tokens. They would then stamp the outside of this container with a seal, not unlike the way we seal envelopes with wax.

We've now reached the phase that brings us to the creation of the tablet. Which is founded upon a truly brilliant idea. The tokens were used to stamp the outsides of the containers as well, to make it clear what they held inside—as if to say, "here within is a bill for five sheep." As time passed, the container would begin to flatten from the repeated pressure of the tokens, moving from the three-dimensional realm of a sphere into the two-dimensional realm of a flat surface. "All right then, so what?" you're probably thinking.

And my response to you is that we are here witnessing the birth of the most important epigraphic surface for cuneiform writing, and not only. Here, in this object, is born the medium for all writing—the prototype, indestructible as diamond. Water alone can alter or annul it. Here is born the tablet.

And with it, the seed of the very thing that you're holding in your hands right now: a book or an e-reader, and the precursor to our smartphones. Here, in 3200–2900 BCE (note the uncertainty of the dates!), is born the mother of all technology, the archetypal handheld device. Our means of communication. Here is the moment in history when information is, at last—and quite literally—at our fingertips.

Under this theory, it's also held that the heavy, bulky

forms of the tokens used to stamp the tablets, as a means of accounting, are connected to the figurative and iconic signs with which writing begins ("pictographic," we might say, but you already know how ambiguous a definition that can be).* And this is where the problems begin. I'll mention only a couple here, which alone are enough to render this theory controversial. Even if it's true that the tokens' marks on the tablets were used for counting, it's not true that their forms, the impressions they made, are identical to writing's first signs. A few are merely similar, such as the sheep impression, for example. One other problem is that the tokens' forms remained the same from 8000 BCE until the beginning of writing, around 3200. It's unlikely that the token-stamps would go unchanged for millennia, across such a vast geographic territory, only to then morph into the signs of a pre-cuneiform writing system.

If these problems related to form aren't enough to dissuade you, there's still an underlying issue with the theory's method, which blends numbers and letters, claiming that the latter descend directly from the former. A direct lineage from numbers to letters: this is perhaps the theory's most insurmountable problem, its true weak link. To stuff the world of letters into the realm of numbers and insert them on the same evolutionary path, to stir them into the same pot, is to force a connection—it's a last-ditch effort to make things tidy, to stretch a bedsheet that's just too short.

Counting is not writing, and tokens are not signs. It's difficult to reconstruct such complex processes using such a mechanistic model. And it's just as difficult to imagine

---

* A pictogram is not a means of linguistic expression—it represents only a primitive phase of drawing-signs, which may or may not have been used to articulate spoken language.

the march toward the invention of writing as an inexorable journey across the millennia, over an enormous swath of earth, an infinite trudge. I don't know about you, but the idea brings me a touch of agoraphobia. The road to writing is long, yes, but it's also winding. And we can explain it without relying on the history of numbers.

SILENT MOVIOLA

Let's watch a movie, now, why don't we? We'll call it a "feature-length" film, the way they used to, since this one lasts for centuries. Subtitles appear on the screen: *Uruk, the first city, southern Mesopotamia.* A close-up of the first tablets. The tokens' impressions in the clay are clearly recognizable: here we have the precursors to numbers. Ones, tens, and hundreds. They're identical to the number signs we'll find in the fully developed cuneiform system. In this aspect, at least, the tokenist theory was on the mark.

Now: a tracking shot of numeric figures, rows of different wedge-shape characters, a complete numeric system. Let's pause the image on the few—the very few—ideographic signs: at this stage, the population is beginning to count, to regulate calculation. But not yet to write. Flash forward. We're now in the beginning of the fourth millennium BCE, during phases IV–III of the Uruk period. Something mind-blowing occurs. And I say mind-blowing because we can follow its evolution step by step. Our film is in slow-mo now—a Moviola of new signs, blooming into view on the clay. These are our icons. *Things.* The protagonist has arrived. But where did it come from?

Not from the tokens and their system of numeric figures. Our protagonist is born from something that was already present—the long, figurative tradition that we find on seal stones. These symbols combine according to iconographic schemes; they become stories, form narrative structures. They trace a plot. And it's from this plot that the first "pictograms" arise: from the crucible of art, from iterated and reiterated forms, from repetition. And not from the cauldron of numbers.

Leap forward another few centuries. We're now in Jemdet Nasr, farther north. Icons start to combine with numbers. We're nearing the end of the film. Icons and numbers unite, and this stable, fruitful marriage is turned toward one purpose alone: to keep the Mesopotamian bureaucratic machine running. The rules for writing numbers grow more complex, adapting to sustain this new city's economy. Tablets appear by the thousands. The signs seem to indicate official roles and professions. The Leviathan of control has awoken. The system is a go. We have our happy ending. But we're still missing our co-star—the villain of the film, in this case. Language.

And there may be no filling this absence. Note that this writing system is not cuneiform—it's still figurative, iconic, even if there are abstract elements (fig. 17). In terms of writing, we're in a primitive phase, defined as "proto," since there are still two fundamental things we don't know: if these signs have phonetic values and, if they do, which language they record. Proto-cuneiform is a mystery. The simplest solution would be to say that the language behind it is Sumerian, the most ancient Mesopotamian language. To assume a different language would be a break in continuity, a shift, and that's tough to identify. But we don't yet find linguistic elements: the first evidence of a grammar dates to

17. Tablet with pictographic cuneiform characters

around 2800 BCE, at least four centuries after the invention of proto-cuneiform. And a lot can happen in four hundred years, can't it?

It's a plot hole we've been struggling to patch for a while now, our missing villain. And in this endless film, this slow-motion picture, what we're watching is a frame-by-frame Moviola of writing's invention. Only there's no sound. It's a silent film. The lack of precise linguistic notations and grammatical connections renders it voiceless.

Of course, nothing prevented cuneiform from flowering and expanding shortly thereafter, but this was possible only because it had already tied its fate to administration. It had attached itself—had glommed on, you might say—to the idea of control. And let's really take a look at this "silent" phase. Think about a more modern form of invoicing, such as bills—do you find any grammar, syntax, or other complex linguistic elements? Not likely. You don't need to be a wordsmith to ask for money. It's the format of the text, how the information is grouped, that reveals its purpose.

It's no secret where to look on a bill to find out how much you owe. Same story with the proto-cuneiform tablets. The form *is* the content. It's all right there, unmistakable. So let the lines and columns do their thing—that's where your eye falls anyway. And close your tab, because this movie's over. Roll credits.

THE AMBIGUOUS REBUS

The beginnings of Sumerian notation were strictly logographic, meaning that they dealt only with representing isolated words, whether verbs, nouns, or adjectives. To give you an example, the Sumerian word for "to write" is *sar*, which also means "plant." And we've already encountered the term *gi* for "cane," which also meant "to reimburse." These are two instances of the rebus that we find rather early on in cuneiform's history, just after the "proto" stage. Sumerian words tend to consist of single syllables; the logograms therefore carry both the word's meaning and the phonetic value expressed in a syllable. For example, the logogram KU_6 is shaped like a fish and also carries the syllabic value *ku*, meaning "fish" in Sumerian.* This syllable *ku* can be used to form other words as well. Double meanings, anyone? *Sign* me up. The high frequency of monosyllables in Sumerian helped make this an easy trick, which was employed often, as we've found.

One drawback, however, resulting directly from Sumerian's monosyllabic nature, is that everything becomes a

---

* In transliteration, signs with a homophonic letter are differentiated by adding a subscript number. (KU_6 tells us that there are five other KUs with different graphic forms.)

little ambiguous. How do you tell, for example, if the word means to "write" or "plant" when the term for both is the same? Or what to do with the word for "water," *a*, which in Sumerian also indicates the locative case (denoting one's presence in a place, like the French word *chez*, or the Latin *apud*)? "Well," you might say, "you can tell from the context." But Sumerians were precise and context didn't cut it. To distinguish between different categories, they created another kind of word: determinatives.

Determinatives are signs that go unread, since they serve only to indicate a semantic class, the category to which a certain logogram belongs. Trees, plants, and wooden objects, for example, are all preceded by the sign for "wood"; cities by the logogram for "city," *uru*; gods by the logogram *dingir*, "divinity." This technique allows us to disambiguate the meaning without tearing our hair out. We simply add a logogram to clarify the subject matter at hand. And if it seems like the rebus is a device common to all invented scripts, from Chinese to Egyptian, the same goes for this category of silent determinatives. From this element alone, for all its ingenuousness, one can get an idea of just how incomplete linguistic notation was in the early days. And that's across the board, not just in Mesopotamia. It consisted merely of strings of words, each one all but isolated.

Only in the next phase do Sumerian's grammatical elements begin to appear. No writing system has ever been invented, or used at any point in time, to perfectly imitate spoken language and all its myriad functions. When it comes to first steps, scripts are just like babies, leaning on chairs and windowsills, groping for anything to help maintain their balance: these supports are an extension of the baby's legs. It's the same with notations in Sumerian. Nouns, a verb here and there, the rare adjective—all are extensions of spoken language, mnemonic devices, means of combating the fallibility of our memories. The chairs and doorjambs of a toddler learning to walk.

UNITED NATIONS

> "But they're mere wedges!"
> —*Enmerkar and the Lord of Aratta* (Sumerian text)

And after that? After that, the toddler takes off running. But beginnings are always mythic, covered in an almost dreamlike patina, where everything feels muffled, some details coming through clear and precise, others remaining vague. An old trick of distant memories, appearing rosier than reality. We've all fallen for it. Even the Mesopotamians.

It was Enmerkar, king of Uruk, who invented the script, in order to send a long message to his rival, the lord of Aratta. When Aratta receives the letter, inscribed on a tablet, he exclaims the words in the above epigraph in disbelief. Enmerkar has caught him off guard, taking a 1–0 lead in a battle of wits. The text that recounts this anecdote comes from a later period, the second millennium BCE, and it does just what memories do: it coats the script's invention, now in the distant past, in a mythological patina. As the myth has it, the wedges were a precise form of communication even from the earliest days—though we all know that cuneiform developed gradually, and that its origins are very different.

With the arrival of phonetic notation, when sounds began to take precedence—from 2800 BCE on—signs could at last break free from their figurative chains and shed the requirement of representing real objects. The Sumerians gave up the pointed stylus and began using one that was wedge-tipped. And they schematized the entire graphic system, doing away with curved lines. This shedding of iconicity took place all in a matter of three hundred years, give or take. Cuneiform ceased to be something "proto." No longer was it composed of instantly recognizable signs: it became cuneiform 2.0, from head to heels (or wedges?). In this new phase, abstract signs and a complex inventory reigned supreme. But there were other problems. Sumerian is an isolated language, with no close relatives, an orphaned only child. It's also an agglutinative language—with re-buses, open syllables, and signs that are deeply invested in their roles. So what would happen if another language took its place? How would it adapt? The short answer is "with difficulty." And here is the long answer (which you can skip, if you'd like, but you'll miss two or three things about world languages).

(Begin digression into historical linguistics.)

The world of languages is divided into just a few large families.

Fusional languages, like all European languages (from Latin to German and everything in between, excluding Basque, Finnish, and Hungarian), are languages that inflect and conjugate nouns and verbs with multivalent suffixes. For example, the ending -us, in Latin's second declension, tells us three things: gender, number, and case (e.g., domi-nus: masculine, singular, subject of the sentence).

The Semitic languages, too, are part of this macro-family, even if only distantly related. Languages like Hebrew and Aramaic have roots made up of three consonants, broken up by vowels and other prefixes and suffixes that determine the word's function. For example, the Akkadian root *prs*, "to decide," becomes *apparas*, "I decide"—with the *a* strategically positioned between the consonants.

Agglutinative languages, on the other hand, like modern Turkish and Sumerian, have monovalent suffixes, one attached to another, in a string. Even Sumerian's roots function in this way, with no internal alterations, in fixed clusters of words pressed one against the other. Clearly the two families I've described here are structurally very different from each other. And there are other families, too, such as the polysynthetic languages, which are even more complex than the agglutinative languages—but we'll leave those be.

Just imagine what might happen if cuneiform—rigged with the monosyllabic and unalterable machinery of Sumerian—were adopted to record a Semitic language, in which the vowels and consonants alternate to create flexible, agile, and pirouetting patterns. Good heavens! And yet that's precisely what happened. Around 2300 BCE, King Sargon defeated the king of Uruk, Lugal-zage-si, and transferred the capital to the city of Akkad, on the Euphrates. Akkad is a city that remains undiscovered—a city that left no trace. When it comes to its language, however, the language of Akkad, we have a superabundance of evidence. Thousands and thousands of tablets. Akkadian falls under the Semitic family, and the cuneiform system was forced to adapt to its variations, to the tango of its vowels and consonants.

In the process of adapting this system to a new language, they had first to make the Sumerian logograms more flexible. Enter syllabograms—numerous and domineering.

Akkadian, with its complex system of roots, is a language in desperate need of flexible syllables, and the minimal selection offered by Sumerian wasn't cutting it. Think about a complex verb such as *aštanapparakkim* (from the root *špr*), which in Akkadian means "I will continue to write to you" (as Enmerkar threatens the lord of Aratta). The verb's root is triconsonantal—to write it out syllabically we'd need a whole heap of syllables: *aš-ta-na-ap-pa-ra-ak-ki-im*. Tapping into the logogram's syllabic potential is of crucial importance, especially when tasked with writing foreign names that must be accurately notated. This suggests that the syllables are flexible by nature, since they must appear not only in the "natural" sequence (consonant + vowel) but also the other way around (vowel + consonant), or else in even more complex sequences (consonant + vowel + consonant).

Add to that, Akkadian uses sounds that don't exist in Sumerian, like the ṣ sound (pronounced like the *z* in *pizza*). This problem is quickly resolved, using none other than the rebus. For example, the logogram *giš* means "wood" in Sumerian, which in Akkadian is *iṣum*. To adapt, the logogram takes on the additional function of the Akkadian syllable *iṣ*, applying it to other similar sounds as well, like *is* and *iz*. Now imagine a similar process for nearly six hundred signs, with rampant redundancies of polyphonic signs (the syllable *ni*, for example, can be represented by six graphically different signs) and homophonic signs (the same sign can carry multiple phonetic values, all completely different from one another, as is the case with *ni*, *né*, *lí*, *lé*, *ì*, *zal*). Not a system known for its economy, in other words.

(End digression into historical linguistics.)

Despite these complications, the adaptation of cuneiform to Akkadian proved miraculously successful—not only did it manage to get off the ground, within a century or two it spread throughout the Middle East, eventually helping to notate numerous languages: Eblaite, Elamite, Old Persian, Hurrian, Hittite, Palaic, Luwian, Ugaritic, Urartian. And others still, but these should suffice. A host of different languages, all bowing to one single writing system: cuneiform is a translinguistic, transnational, and transgeographical passe-partout. The true emperor of the Middle East. But behind every great emperor is a great consort. And in this case that consort is the language of Akkad.

The marriage between cuneiform and the Akkadian language remained strong and stable for centuries, facilitating communication at the highest levels. Every empire of the Bronze Age (Hittite, Assyro-Babylonian, Egyptian, and others) carried out international relations, economic exchanges, diplomacy, and royal chitchat all thanks to the help of Akkadian cuneiform. We can imagine the messengers, armed with engraved tablets, traveling across deserts and streams, mountains and seasons, taking down responses on their arrival, gathering the gripes of spoiled kings—back and forth, caravan after caravan. For centuries. For the entirety of the second millennium BCE this marriage functioned, the nations united by a sole method of communication—though not mass communication. It was a tool reserved for the global elite (or as much of the globe as was then known). The cultural and economic nerve centers, the United Nations of the Bronze Age, the consequential decisions, the wars—all were woven together by Akkadian wedges. Just like French in the Napoleonic Empire, the English of Cool Britannia. And perhaps like Chinese in our future. Which, in fact, reminds me—it's time we made our way to China.

Chinese Turtles

It won't be surprising if the future leads us all to China. At least, I wouldn't be shocked. China invented the longest-lasting and most stable writing system in history. Chinese—the language—as we know it today is almost the same as the first inscriptions from nearly 3,200 years ago. And Chinese—the script—is the only system in the world still used to represent the language for which it was invented. A sturdy foundation, and an indomitable synergy, resistant to all overtures of change. The Chinese script cannot be budged—for millennia it has remained proudly the same. And at the same time, complex.

Somehow, someway, even the first grumblings of its existence were remarkable. We've seen how unsteady the first stages were in Egypt and Mesopotamia, how short for words—a phrase here, a phrase there, nothing too complicated. But in China it was highly complex right from the start. We find a fully formed system, a complete repertoire of signs, from the very first moment we encounter it: no proto-, no tag-labels, no numeric tablets with four names carved into them. The first examples of Chinese contain complete sentences, almost all comprehensible. An unprecedented feat.

So does this mean that the Chinese script was invented overnight? That it sprouted like a mushroom at the end of the second millennium BCE, already fully formed? Not likely. Much more probable is that what we're seeing, what you'll see in a moment, is already an advanced stage, far removed (though we don't know how far) from the moment of invention. Its syntax is flexible, the number of characters already substantial—between three thousand and five thousand, all well designed and clear. Hundreds of inscriptions on turtle shells, ox scapulae, and bronze objects, buried in various tombs, concentrated around the capital of the Shang dynasty, Anyang, in northeast-central China.

The question we must ask ourselves about these remains is whether, indeed, they remain only because the inscriptions are found on weather-resistant materials, much less perishable than material like papyrus or parchment. Turtle shells and metal make for perfectly durable surfaces. We might assume that the evidence we have represents only the few lucky survivors—that an incalculable number of inscriptions fell victim to time's voracity, thrown pitilessly down its gullet, never to be seen. A much more realistic scenario, compared with imagining that some hyperliterate scribe, in the court of the Shang dynasty, conceived of something as finished and polished as was the Chinese script in 1200 BCE, all in the blink of an eye.

Assuming, then, that the first phases came earlier, how far back must we date its invention? Scholars have pointed to Neolithic signs as antecedents—signs spread throughout China, from Banpo, in Xi'an, in the west to Liangzhu in the east and dating to about 5000 BCE—though nothing is certain, even if some of the signs resemble those found in Anyang. They're not sufficient, in any case, for re-creating a complete inventory. We can't label a few simple signs, with their crude geometry, a "script." That the eventual script might have grown out of former symbols is by no means an absurd hypothesis—in fact, it's true for other regions—but proving that usage and meaning have remained consistent over the span of millennia is an extremely difficult task. How would you piece it all together? It would be like connecting two dots that are miles apart, with nothing in between to guide you: there's no path, and without a path we're lost.

And the timeline problems don't end there: 1200 BCE is much later than the inventions in Mesopotamia and Egypt. Two millennia later. And two thousand years is a long time. People migrate. Relationships form, even between distant populations. Ideas take root. And even though there's no such evidence in the archaeological record, we must, out of intellectual honesty, ask ourselves whether China invented anything at all. Perhaps some external influence, one of these already literate regions, butted in?

It would be unfair to dispatch this question with a yes or a no. Doubts about possible influences remain. Though perhaps this is just being overcautious. In truth, the case that other cultures left their mark on the Chinese script grows weaker and thinner every year. The script created in China, to state it plainly, is too "Chinese," too particular, sui generis in terms of its structure, to be anything other than a product of its land. By the looks of it, then, China invented writing, just like Mesopotamia and Egypt. Our third invention.

A DISASTER-FREE WEEK?

The first inscriptions were various texts, sometimes up to five hundred lines long, carved into the lower part of a turtle's shell, called the plastron (fig. 18). The plastron is the belly of the shell—a smooth, flat surface, all but asking to be inscribed. We might assume that this surface was chosen for its durability, but the truth is we have no idea what the motive was. Many of these plastrons bear no inscriptions (they're anepigraphic). The mystery of why they chose these objects is essentially impenetrable.

Other inscriptions are found on the shoulder blades of oxen—a much less welcoming surface for writing. They lack the plastron's flatness. And here again we have no sense of why they were chosen as a writing surface. Durability does seem like a prerequisite, but we simply can't rule out the influence of pure chance. We know very little about these objects, but we know a whole lot about what's written on them.

Engraved on these objects are the divination practices of the highest echelon of Chinese society, the royal court of Anyang, and they are attempts to communicate with the

18. Turtle plastron inscribed with Old Chinese

beyond. We here enter the realm of the paranormal, though even in this world, the Chinese followed their own spirit. Modern fortune-tellers, especially in America, use tablets engraved with letters of the alphabet and the numbers 0 to 9—known, of course, as Ouija boards (the name, it would seem, derives from the French *oui* and the German *ja*, an affirmative yes). We've all seen images of people calling questions out to the dead, the triangular pointer sliding across the letters, forming the words of their response—which typically comes in the "he loves me . . . he loves me not" variety, a simple yes or no. Blunt, penetrating answers are the key here. That way the dead don't have to work too hard, and the living can get their kicks.

In Anyang the goal is much the same, though the approach is a bit different, since the method of communication isn't put down in writing straight away. The séance happens first, then comes the engraving of the text. The text is the cherry on top, a means of setting the events in stone, a kind of chronicle. So went divination in the Shang dynasty.

It's most likely that these interrogations were conducted orally. The questions revolved around the king: Will his various endeavors succeed? Will it be a good harvest? What new disasters await us this week? They'd then heat up particular areas of the turtle shell or ox scapula and wait for a crack to form in the surface. That crack was the message, and its shape had to be well defined in order for the response to be valid. Last, they'd carve the text of the question they'd asked aloud directly onto the crack, to elicit a verdict: a positive or negative prophecy. The text was arranged in two vertical columns and followed an almost formulaic pattern: the date, the week (which was ten days long), the type of prophecy, and the name of the functionary who'd asked the question. And then the question itself.

To give you an idea of just how fully articulated and polished this early Chinese was, here's an example plucked at random:

> Five days later, a messenger from the west will certainly arrive with bad news. Zhiguo reports that Tufang attacked his eastern border and seized two settlements. Furthermore, the Gongfang have invaded the lands on our western front.

Imagine an ox bone reporting on two or three weeks of enemy attacks. And along with these divinations came dreams, previsions, sacrifices made in honor of a group of spirits, among which figured their royal ancestors. These are pieces of flash fiction, micro-narratives, facts and figures—a carefully arranged bulletin. All revealing their obsession with dates, auspicious days, favorable circumstances, the magic number. This almanac-like system brings to mind the rituals of the *I Ching*. History occurring and recurring in cycles; traditions that just won't die. Plus ça change . . .

THE GLORIOUS LIFE OF LADY HAO

The history of the Chinese script is tied up with the history of a woman. The tomb of Fu Hao is the most extravagant tomb of the Shang era, and its discovery in 1976 one of the most significant in all of Chinese archaeology. Not only because the tomb was miraculously found sealed and intact, but because of the window it gives us into the glorious life of Fu Hao.

Fu means "lady," and the tomb is dedicated entirely to celebrating her life. Lady Hao was a formidable woman, to say the least. Her position one to which few women in antiquity could ever have aspired. Her tomb overflowing with artifacts in jade (more than seven hundred), bronze (around two hundred), engraved turtle shells. Three hundred and fifty inscriptions of her name. Her entire life contained within. She was one of the sixty-four wives (I kid you not) of Wu Ding, the first of the Shang dynasty's nine kings. But Lady Hao was not just any old wife. From the inscriptions and the weapons found in her tomb, we know that she was a military commander, in charge of multiple campaigns, with thirteen thousand soldiers and several generals under her command. She was the most feared leader of the Shang dynasty, with the gall to face even the dreaded Guifang of the north.

Beyond all this, she was also her husband's attentive advisor. And a professional fortune-teller. The fact that the king gave her this responsibility is testimony to Lady Hao's enormous power, and to just how highly Wu Ding regarded her. Through divination, the king followed his wife's pregnancy, fretting over her health and the health of their unborn child. The king's prognostication is quite interesting. Wu Ding identified two days of the week as being auspicious for giving birth—the turtle shell was covered with cracks, the question posed again and again. And the results? "Three weeks and one day later, on jiayin, the baby was born. It was not good. It was a girl."

In what was very much a man's world, Lady Hao was a unicorn. Not only was she an example of a powerful woman, she was an example of the rarest intellectual fortitude. Lady Hao was an Amazon, a Valkyrie, a dynamic strategist, a priestess, an influential politician. And it was Lady Hao who catalyzed the invention of a new script, shepherding it into being.

I can think of no similar example: a woman who was not only powerful but gifted with such foresight. Boudicca led armies, Queen Victoria simply led, Catherine the Great was a patron of the arts. But Lady Hao had a step on all of them: she understood the value of culture before anyone else, before culture even had a name. Lady Hao saw the future. In our long and male-dominated history, it may well be that Lady Hao is a woman without peer.

DON'T CALL THEM IDEOGRAMS

Earlier I mentioned the particularity of the Chinese script. And indeed, its one-of-a-kind structure is precisely what leads us to believe that we're dealing with an invention and not an idea stolen from others and localized. Chinese, like Sumerian, is rife with monosyllabic words. Prime soil for the rebus. And here is our launching point. Because here is where the Chinese tale begins to diverge, where it takes on its own, unique characteristics, where it becomes multifaceted. We'll start from the determinative stage, known as stage III—when, as in Sumerian, determinatives were used to distinguish between homophonic words.

Let's look at an example. Already in the Bronze Age, the sign for elephant (pronounced *dzjangx*) was being used for a similar-sounding word, *hsiang*, "image," "appearance." The meaning changes, but the sound stays practically the same. Up to this point we're dealing with a rebus, or polysemy. But then another trick is stacked on top: polyphony. Which means that a "pictogram," like the one used for the word *k'ou*, "mouth," can also be used for the word/verb *ming*, "name," "to name/to call": the two words are linked by meaning but not by sound, which makes the sign polyphonic. Right away, we find ourselves in need of two kinds of determinatives: semantic determinatives, tied to meaning; and phonetic determinatives, tied to sound. And here, in this formative moment—when words must be disambiguated both in meaning and in sound—something special occurs.

The determinative fuses with the word and together they become a single entity, integral parts of the same character. This symbiosis produces signs composed of two elements: the original word, with its meaning, and the determinative, whether semantic or phonetic. Taking up our earlier example again, we find that the sign for *hsiang* absorbs a secondary element (in this case the sign for "man") to communicate its second meaning, "image," while for "elephant" the base sign remains unchanged. That's our semantic determinative. For the phonetic determinative, the base sign for "mouth," *k'ou*, takes on an element that gives us the sound *ming*, to specify that we're talking about the verb "to name/to call," pronounced *ming*.

For another example, take a look at the sign 洋, "ocean," which is a combination of the images for "water," 氵, and "sheep," 羊. On the semantic level, obviously, "sheep" has no business being a part of this word, but on the phonetic level it does, since it is pronounced just like "ocean," *yang*. It's a marvelously coherent system, with meaning and sound coming together to form each sign. Like inserting one thing into another with a satisfying *click*.

This fusion, this *click*, is unique. Which is why calling the Chinese script "ideographic" is an indignity, not to mention an error. Though born from drawing, Chinese characters are a means of notating not "ideas" but specific words (morphemes) of the Chinese language, with precise sounds identifiable only with that language. And the system reflects both meaning and pronunciation. It is therefore a logographic-syllabic writing system, based on phono-semantic compounds, at least for 80 percent of its characters. The Chinese language lends itself perfectly to the rebus: it links signs by similar sound, creating polysemy. Through a painstaking process, the system was channeled into its two-part structure of compounds, as in the game mahjong, which after all is based on Chinese characters. Though it's even better than mahjong, since in the game of the Chinese script you have thousands of tiles.

From the turtle-shell period (OBI, which stands for Oracle Bone Inscriptions) to today, we can trace an unbroken lineage. The sign for a cultivated field, for mouth, for turtle, for horse, eye, elephant, mountain, fire, and many others still bear evidence of their graphic origins, from the very beginning, in 1200 BCE. Today their forms are different, but the strong influence of their underlying icons remains clear. This resistance, this tight bond with the objects being represented, and with the precision of their sounds, is extraordinary, and it is the source of this script's true power. And this first phase is even more extraordinary for how regimented it already is, how neatly classified, with everything in its right place. The sound-meaning symbiosis and the determinative that completes it resemble the well-trained legions of Lady Hao, who dispatched her enemies in an orderly fashion.

Maybe Chinese will be the language of the future, maybe it won't. Either way, it's highly unlikely that the script itself will propagate. Not only because it feels so complex and foreign to the Western world, but because it would have to overcome centuries of uncontested rule by the alphabet. The opposite is much more plausible—that pinyin, alphabetical Chinese (known also as "Romanized" Chinese), will spread in tandem with the language. Regardless, it's no surprise that such an icon-based script has served as an anchor for the Chinese language, over millennia of uninterrupted use, with an almost militant resistance to change. Whatever the destiny of the Chinese script on the global scale, in China it will most certainly hold its ground, bound to the art of calligraphy and crystallized in its aesthetic harmony. It may not conquer the world, but its resistant and imperious iconicity can help us explain something else: the trajectory along which we find ourselves moving today, all throughout the world. The truth is that we're hopelessly drawn to iconicity: icons have an undeniable gravitational force when it comes to scripts. We'll talk more about this soon—but what I will say now, and without reservation, is that the future of signs lies in images.

Across the Ocean

IT COULD HAVE GONE WORSE

We've made it to the final invention. The final story. A story that fought hard to claim its place in the annals of written language. We'll have to sail a ways from China, and dock our boat in Mexico.

The Mesoamerican scripts are the most recent invention, if—out of caution or personal opinion—we're excluding Easter Island's Rongorongo. For the Mayan script to claim its title as a true invention, it took hundreds of years and a painstaking process of decipherment. Less than two generations ago, its glyphs were seen as a limited mnemonic system, with no structure to its phonetic notation.* An uncodified mess, in other words.

It's no secret that the attitude around glyphs was a little prejudiced. We're an ocean away from Europe, in an environment long viewed as barely civilized. It was par for the course, this Old World snobbism, looking down on the New World with the pitying, paternalistic gaze of one who's seen it all, invented it all. As one of my colleagues is

---

* Ignace Gelb, in his important *A Study of Writing* (1963), holds that Mayan cannot be phonetic because, at that point, the script had yet to be deciphered, despite the fact that various Mayan dialects were still being spoken in the modern age.

always saying, with the same mistrust toward anyone who dares conceive of a new idea: "Eh, nothing's ever invented." And yet . . . In the Middle Preclassic period (900–500 BCE), amid a profusion of Olmec imagery, a revolution was under way. And I know *revolution* is the kind of word that people are always tossing around to grab attention, but in this case it's actually true. A true revolution was in the works.

But one step at a time. Let's start from the beginning. Diego de Landa was a fiendish, merciless, and highly determined man—a Franciscan bishop sent toward the middle of the sixteenth century to forcefully convert the peoples of the Yucatán.* So thoroughly did he ingratiate himself with the local population, they had little fear in showing him their most prized possession: the Mayan codices. In the eyes of the diabolic Diego de Landa, these writings could be nothing more than lies, superstition, manifestations of the devil. He had nearly all of them burned. However, like any true fiend, he set about studying that which he was destroying, producing an almost ethnographic work on their script. He interrogated the descendants of the Maya and quizzed them on the phonetic properties of what they were reading. Before long, he convinced himself that the script was alphabetical, albeit with a few inconsistences and redundancies. Something about his method wasn't squaring, but he'd laid the foundations.

It would take hundreds of years, and a man more fiendish than any James Bond villain (though with a sharp

---

* The etymology of Yucatán, true or alleged, is already enough to make us wary of the relationship between proselytizers and the locals. *Yucatán* comes from the Maya *tectetan*, "I don't understand," or from *uyutan*, *uyukatan*, or *yukutan*, meaning "hear how they talk." Perhaps here, too, we're dealing with the patina of myth, but so be it.

mind, here pictured [fig. 19] with a cat), before we'd determine that the Mayan script is not based on an alphabetical system as de Landa thought, nor is it some structureless, iconographic mnemonic device. Mayan is a syllabary, a logo-syllabary to be precise. Yuri Knorozov—Russian, soldier, linguist—had the good sense to build on de Landa's work, which wasn't all that bad, refining his phonetic approach and eventually recognizing a substantial number of syllables.

This shift in approach was the true first step toward decipherment. But the air surrounding these glyphs was still toxic. Are you sure they really constitute a script? I mean, just look at them, carved into the walls of monuments and

19. The linguist Yuri Knorozov, with cat

important buildings—you can tell something's majorly off: Don't they seem, deep down, like mere iconographic narratives? With a certain coherence, yes, but nonetheless still just drawings, decorations. Such was the suspicion that slithered among the "glyphologists" of the day (or "glyphers," as Linda Schele called them, herself a towering figure in Mayan's decipherment). And the most suspicious of all was J. Eric S. Thompson, a pioneer among the experts, who'd already created a cataloguing system for the glyphs, assigning each a T number (T for Thompson, as it was later defined—did I mention that philologists are often self-oriented?).

And, of course, it was his ego that began to weigh down the decipherment process. Thompson was convinced that Mayan, at its core, was a logographic system, lacking phonetic notation, and that Knorozov's method was therefore invalid. Thompson was also convinced that the Maya were a virtuous people, devoted to moderation and temperance. And he was wrong about that, too.

No—in civilization, as in writing systems, there's no such thing as purity. Knorozov understood this. No script is composed solely of logograms. Even our paltry alphabet (paltry in its number of characters, that is) uses logograms, such as numbers and other signs like %, $, &, @. The myopic Sir Eric! Our Russian cat-lover, on the other hand, was clever enough to make use of the Mayan languages that were already known and still spoken in modern times, and to rely on the easily recognizable iconicity of certain logograms, such as those for turkey and dog, which are linked to a syllabic spelling of the Mayan words for "turkey" and "dog." And Knorozov discovered many others—not all correctly, but his method worked.

This is a virtuous story, one that led, albeit with a few

obstacles, to a successful conclusion. And it also serves as a cautionary tale. We should never put our blind faith in what we read in books, and we should never trust scholars as if they're gurus. It's essential that we trust our own critical instinct. If we'd listened to the ipse dixits of the holier-than-thous, the solipsistic experts; if we'd taken it for granted that America had, in the end, invented nothing at all; if, in short, we'd paid too much mind to Thompson, we'd never have managed to decipher Mayan. And let's not forget that this success story is owed not to the glory of some lone hero but to a decades-long effort by a team of scholars, fusing their various talents, constantly testing and calibrating their findings. Success, I repeat, is invariably founded upon collaboration. It could have gone worse.

FALSE START, LONG LIFE

Even though the Mayan script dominated the entire pre-Hispanic era—before the arrival of the conquistadors in Central America (1519 CE)—it nevertheless is not the most ancient Mesoamerican script that we know of. Thousands of years earlier, around 500 BCE, and perhaps even a century or two before then, another writing system left its mark. We have only a telescopic view of it, since it counts among the most enigmatic scripts in the world (and by "enigmatic," of course, I mean undeciphered), but already present in this script are the seeds of what's to come, the pre-Mayan ingredients, though almost all illegible. Let's spin our telescope around to get a closer look.

In the Oaxaca Valley, at Monte Albán (c. 600–500 BCE), we find the Zapotec script—incomplete, a rough draft, though already reminiscent of the two obsessions that would come to define the Mayan culture: calendars and blood. In the New World's first known instance of writing, on a stone known as a danzante (Monument 2 at San José Mogote, Oaxaca [fig. 20]), we find the image of a slain and bloody captive with two glyphs between his legs—his name, perhaps. He's in a bad way, the poor fellow, and he's surrounded by three hundred other bloodied captives. As for the writing? Still a mystery.

As if the Zapotec script wasn't enough, it has a cousin, a few miles to the east, to compound our headache. A script known as "Isthmian." Not a very imaginative name, but it gets the idea across, since the script comes from the Isthmus of Tehuantepec, the shortest distance between the Gulf

20. Stela of a danzante at Monte Albán, Mexico

of Mexico and the Pacific Ocean. A serpent of land, lapped by the sea. The Isthmian script is also known, inaccurately, as the Epi-Olmec script, since some contend that it's derived from the preceding Olmec culture, which serves as a foundation and was flourishing as early as 1500 BCE. But the term is misleading: it'd be like calling the Etruscans "epi-Romans." Best to give it a neutral, geographic name and call it "Isthmian."

The preceding Olmec phase, however—at sites like La Venta and San Lorenzo—gave rise to several traditions that would last into the succeeding Mayan civilization. There are two things we should point out about the Olmecs, since both are traditions that will endure for centuries and that will be ardently adopted by the Maya. The first is their boundless bloodlust. They weren't violent, at least not according to the historical record, but drawing blood was extremely important for the Olmecs. Chopping off penises and tongues in public was a powerful symbolic ceremony, for preserving the social and cosmic order. The practice was grounded in myth, a belief in palingenesis. The gods had gifted life to men, sacrificing body parts and blood, and therefore blood needed to be returned to the gods. Blood meant life. So bring on the mutilation, torture, and gore.

The second fact is more pedestrian, literally. The Olmecs were the first to invent a game using a ball. An incredibly long tradition, still played today in the region—a game that is now called ulama, and is not all that different from squash, though don't assume that it was merely recreational. The game had ritual and symbolic aspects, sometimes including human sacrifice. Historically, these sacrifices came later, toward the end of the Mayan period, but the moral is the same: blood must be spilled, even when playing ball, in this case via fervent decapitations. We know as much from the *Popol Vuh*, a text that recounts the mythical origins of the K'iche' Maya of Guatemala, and which leads us to believe that they may have used the decapitated heads as balls. We don't know for sure, but it'd be grand if it were true.

The Isthmian script seems to emerge from this Olmec atmosphere of ball games, decapitations, and blood. But enough splatter, already. In Isthmian, as in the Zapotec script, we witness the appearance of the calendar. In the few Isthmian texts to have survived (only ten or so), we find elements related to calculations and to the order of time—subjects of widespread interest in the classic period. Like the Tuxtla Statuette, for example (fig. 21). Take a careful look. Covering its front, back, and sides are various texts that appear to be (but aren't) Mayan glyphs—what they are, instead, are numbers in a "long count." They're dates.* We find them on Stela C at Tres Zapotes as well, engraved with the date 32 BCE, and on the splendid La Mojarra Stela, from the second century CE (fig. 22).

One need only glance at these inscriptions to understand a fundamental aspect of the early Mesoamerican period: it was by no means a beginning, but already an advanced phase of writing. Sound a little like China? The first traces of Isthmian already constitute a complex script, able to codify extensive texts. Which would point us to antecedents. It's a kind of false start. The true beginning, the earliest trace,

* The Mayan Long Count was a nonrepeating numbering system used for keeping track of the days, with a structure that varied according to each numeral's position. The first (the "ones") was base-20, the second (the "tens") base-18, the third and fourth again base-20, the fifth base-13. The Long Count's complete cycle was therefore 20 x 18 x 20 x 20 x 13 = 1,872,000 days (nearly 5,125 years). Year zero, the calendar's starting point, corresponds to August 13, 3113 BCE. Now you know why the world was supposed to end in 2012.

21. The Tuxtla Statuette, Veracruz, Mexico

22. La Mojarra Stela, Veracruz, Mexico

thanks to the whims of archaeology, is invisible. Isthmian is the New World's first script, but don't kid yourself that we can actually read it: it remains an undeciphered system. No matter what the rumors are. Years ago, a decipherment of the inscriptions at La Mojarra was published to media fanfare urbi et orbi—only to be dismantled in the blink of an eye, by experts far more rigorous than your fly-by-night decipherer. When it comes to method, as we'll see, there's very little wiggle room.

EMOJIS

The signs in the Isthmian and Mayan scripts resemble one another, and so, too, do their internal structures. The earliest Mayan inscriptions date to around the birth of Christ; the most recent are from sixteen centuries later. A highly durable writing system, and one filled with a good deal of creativity and imagination, as we'll see.

Its structure is logo-syllabic, with hundreds of signs in its inventory (a base of nearly 250, with at least 500 logograms). The signs can carry the value of both a logogram and a syllabogram: the same glyph can be used for both functions. Which means that, to all effects, each text is charged with double meaning. To give you an idea of just how well developed its structure was, let's look at an example using one of its most delightful glyphs—the glyph for cacao. Chocolate was sacred, the drink of the gods, a mixture of cacao and spices.

But what matters to us is the sign (fig. 23) and how it functions. As a whole it indicates the word *kakau*, and the individual elements, its constituent parts, are what allow

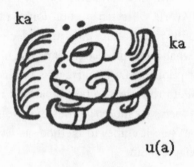

23. Mayan sign for "chocolate"

24. Another Mayan sign for "chocolate"

us to read it. This reading is syllabic. The syllable *ka* is repeated and combined with the syllable *u(a)*, in which the *a* is a redundant vowel, though Mayan notates it all the same, picking up the *a* from the preceding syllable. The cherry, or cherries, on top, are the two dots just above the figure. These alert us to the phonetic reduplication, letting us know that we need to read *ka* twice. The Maya weren't fiddling around—even the tiniest of dots counted.

Evident, as well, is the complete artistic freedom they showed in their graphic interpretations of the signs: if I were to tell you that the glyph for cacao could also be represented using this variant (fig. 24), you might be skeptical. The base sign/icon is a fish, which gives us the syllable *ka*. That these two signs could indicate the same word seems almost incredible. And yet—did you notice the two dots, over on the left? There they are, unmistakable.

And this is just one example, not even among the most complex. The paleographic variants are astonishing: syllables flip around, creating impossible-to-recognize configurations, the logograms confound, sign after sign looks like a face. Glance below at the variants for the word *witz*, meaning "mountain" (fig. 25). The first sign is known as the "head variant," depicting a face, the second is the logogram, the third the logogram with a phonetic complement, the fourth a syllabic rendering.

It's enough to drive you mad—yet this incomprehensible pattern did nothing to stop the decipherers from unlocking Mayan's secrets. If the human mind can conceive of such imaginative work, the human mind can decipher it, too. I may complain about Cretan Hieroglyphic, but with Mayan there's nothing to do but turn and run. First off, it lacks something that might have aided in the early phases of decipherment, something we'd expect to find, given the path followed by other invented scripts. And that something is . . . wait for it . . . the rebus. We find almost no trace of it in Mayan. Which is very strange. The only explanation would

WITZ   WITZ   wi-WITZ   wi-tzi

25. The signs for "mountain," *witz* in Mayan

be that Mayan is in fact a secondary invention, derived from the undeciphered Isthmian script. But that's not something we know for sure. The dates of Mayan's beginnings are always shifting. It may well be that the rebus is hiding in some earlier phase that we can't see; should we discover more inscriptions, it could help clear things up.

There's one other factor separating Mayan from all other early scripts, which you may have noticed even just glancing at the examples. Animate and inanimate things are all represented as if they were living: faces, unidentifiable beings with eyes and mouths, animal heads, signs indicating the part for the whole (pars pro toto, in technical jargon, such as legs, arms, feet, hands). And all of those head variants, like the signs for the numbers between one and nineteen, are represented by faces. Isn't this a little odd? If you ask me, it all bears the stamp of Olmec iconography—though whether Olmec or not, this headstrong fixation on depicting living things and their parts is without parallel. Mayan glyphs live and breathe and speak.

I know what's swirling around in your head right now. I can read your mind like Lady Hao. Emojis. But they aren't the same. Mayan signs carry a specific phonetic value. They're syllables or logograms. The little yellow faces we send to our friends are completely ideographic, though they're little faces nonetheless, that much we can agree upon. We still need to figure out how Mayan became so emoji-fied, on the graphic level. And there might be an explanation.

LIVING SOULS

All Mesoamerican scripts are obsessed with iconicity, and not only do they feature it prominently, they safeguard it for the future. Why? There's always some existential cause at the bottom of things. The signifier (that is, the sign) is bound, inextricably, to the essence of the signified. Vitality seeps from every pore of an object once it's inscribed. The sign is a living thing. Whoever writes animates the inanimate, gives it life, spirit, as if the material and the spiritual were one and the same. For Italians, and to a large extent for Americans, immersed in the Christian tradition as we are—though we may not recognize it or even wish it so—the spiritual and the material are two separate things, with the material existing on a lower plane (see, for instance, a phenomenon such as iconoclasm, which aims to destroy the material). Any union between the two always feels a little strange.

For the Maya, though, it's not just the body and soul that are alive, *things* are alive, too. Just look at the jade objects from the Olmec period, which are infused with breath. Carved into their chests, in line with the lungs and heart, is a T-shaped symbol, one of the most ancient signs—meaning wind. And from this T they breathe. Look at their belt plaques, too, with pendants shaped like the heads and names of ancestors, which alternate to form a kind of talking dance. Which is all to say that, in Mesoamerica, what's written speaks. And it's no coincidence that their head-shaped inscriptions are turned toward the direction in which they're read, as if they're truly engaged in dialogue with the reader.

And displaying these heads, for the Maya, required a certain amount of monumentality. Stone stelae, altars, panels, public declarations of royal deeds, lineages, and superhuman ancestors. Brilliantly colored panels advertising the king's authority. All infused with life. And all proof of the incredible power of decipherment. Up until half a century ago, Mayan glyphs were still seen as flat drawings, the script still not considered to be phonetic. Then, in a matter of a few years, that view was turned on its head. Mayan glyphs are so phonetic that they're heavily, redundantly full of sound, and they have been since the first Isthmian inscriptions. Mayan glyphs speak and, unlike Chinese and cuneiform signs, are also infused with spirit. In an adjective, they're alive.

End of Story

I've now told two sweeping stories. The first set on islands, filled with unresolved enigmas and freely drawn borders, no more definite than those of the islands themselves, whose forms change according to the whims of the wind and water. A story filled not only with secret but with wonder, and the hope and excitement for all that we'll one day discover. The potential of decipherment. Then there's our second story, more closely tied to cities, to empires, to government and celebration. Two grand stories, whose protagonist, writing, is not always so indispensable. Though it's a character that, once invented, becomes magically necessary, and allows the society that adopts it to make a quantum leap forward. At times it takes on its role reluctantly, as a kind of Zelig, and gains depth only as it settles into the part. It just needs a good director, someone to give it space, to let it find its voice.

With the exception of Chinese, the scripts we've looked at so far are done for, dead. Cuneiform lasted nearly four thousand years, Egyptian three thousand and it was gone. With Mayan it's harder to say, somewhere around two thousand years, and the script would have certainly lasted longer had not the conquistadors arrived to wipe the slate clean. Thousands of years of usage, transmission, diffusion. For the island scripts, life was even shorter, but they wore their centuries well. And even though social complexity can live and endure without writing, the city or state's thirst for control is a powerful catalyst in ensuring its longevity. Writing systems flourish when they're channeled toward a common aim, when their potential appreciates over time, when they sense a reason for their existence. Invention lies in optimizing your discovery.

Which is why we must think of invention as a process of gradual, layered formation, from the spark of wordplay to the creation of a complete catalogue of signs, an agreed-upon set that can be passed down from generation to generation: in short, a multistep trajectory from discovery to invention. We shouldn't be surprised, then, that all paths of development for *new* writing systems follow very similar formative trajectories. And here you have them.

1. ICONICITY: All of the earliest, foundational scripts arise from a set of figurative signs that depict "things" from the natural world, or from that particular culture. Levels of stylization vary, but iconicity is always present, and in some cases, as in Mayan and Egyptian, it endures for centuries. Art seems to function as the springboard for a script's invention: repeated icons, a coherent narrative, *storytelling*— these are the first steps toward putting sound to paper, so to speak. The pathways aren't always identical, and I don't want to simplify things too much, but the underlying iconic structure is always there. And it's an unwritten law that, in the early days of a script, the logograms will change from icons to symbols and they'll never go back or move in the opposite direction. An irreversible passage—entropic, almost.

2. SYLLABLE: Syllables are the natural armor of sounds. All early writing systems operate on a syllabic structure.* For Sumerian and Chinese this is dogma, given the vast amount of monosyllabic words in their vocabularies. Syllable = word = sign. Though, as we've seen, this aspect may be less linguistic than it is "biological." For evidence, just look to some of the more recently invented scripts (even if they're secondary inventions, that is, with minor outside influences) such as Bamum in Cameroon, Cherokee in North America, Woleai in the Caroline Islands, Afaka in Suriname. All syllabic systems. The syllable is our most salient unit of sound, our most spontaneous, holistic utterance. If you don't believe me, start reciting the alphabet out loud: *a*, *b*, *c*, *d*. Keep going, now, syllable by syllable.

3. LIMITED SYNTAX: And finally, as we know, things happen gradually. At least in the case of gradual inventions, those that we can reconstruct from their very beginnings, from the first written word, like cuneiform and Egyptian. It starts as a trickle, not as a torrent of epic poetry or scientific treatises. We see timid approaches at linguistic notation, painstaking progress, portholes into the world of spoken language, lists of words, inventories, labels. Few verbs, minimal syntax. Incompleteness, limited functionality. But herein lies the beauty: recognizing the potential of these attempts and creating strategies to expand them. To record a verb or an abstract noun requires first a rebus, then a syllable. To build a complete catalogue of sign-sounds takes adjusting, cutting, adding, repeating, starting over, defining, disambiguating. A kind

---

* Even with Egyptian hieroglyphs, which have a consonantal base, and therefore seem to be an exception, we can find an interpretation: the presence of many morphemes or monoconsonantal words.

of dressmaking for scripts. In other words, we aren't born with it.

DIDEROT

What we shouldn't do, in thinking about these three aspects, is start talking of them as universal qualities of writing. They're three structural commonalities, nothing more. No need to go about systematizing, creating laws, paving over the unique characteristics. Instead, we must remain faithful to the idea expressed a few pages back and resist the taxonomic temptation to classify everything, to generalize every tendency. There's a reason we went about busting the myth of the all-imposing Leviathan state and reconsidering the concept of necessity, which is often, and misguidedly, linked to the invention of writing. We must continue to view invention as something intrinsically free, spontaneous, and natural, something born from the drive for novelty, not from necessity.

Without novelty, in fact, without the *hunt* for the new, we wouldn't be human beings. This is what our brains are programmed for, that feeling of freshness that new things give us. It's the same feeling you get when you see a glittering dress in the shop window, or a book that's just come out, or a shiny new car. You want it not because you need it, but because the hunt alone sets your blood beating. (Well, maybe we *do* need the book.)

The part of your brain that's involved in this process is called the *substantia nigra*, located in the midbrain, near the hippocampus and the amygdala, which play an important role in learning and memory. When we're exposed to something new, something never before seen, this region lights up and we even get a hit of dopamine, a neurotransmitter associated with new stimuli and the perception of gratification (and with drugs like cocaine).

Dopamine, however, does not provide us with gratification; it merely gives us the motivation to seek it out. It stimulates us, pushes us, but it doesn't provide any instant payoff. It urges us to explore, in the *anticipation* of a reward. Each new stimulus gives us a reason to search, to discover more, to learn more. Indeed, the entire process is linked to learning: the more new information we expose our brains to, the more flexible the hippocampus grows. The more data we amass, the better adapted we are to the world. In evolutionary terms, this ability is essential to our survival.

And not only. It helps with a few bonus things, too, like writing, or the wheel, or TV. Without new experiences, we could never create anything new. We would lack creativity. With no impulse toward novelty there would be no discovery. It seems obvious, but it isn't. It's biological. A chemical trap with its ups and downs, to which we are humble servants. As Diderot's famous dressing gown taught us.* And yet without this trap, without this servitude, there would be no inventions.

* One day, the renowned French author Diderot was given a beautiful dressing gown. When he put it on, however, he realized that it outshone all the other old and dusty objects in his possession. It was too elegant. What to do? He decided to overhaul his wardrobe and furniture, to live up to the gown's standard. The Diderot effect = a trap.

EXPERIMENTS

Tradition

TELEPHONE

To say that an invention, like that of writing, emerged from our biological need for novelty is no stretch of the imagination. But writing is not imprinted in our genes: it is a cultural phenomenon, it must be learned and, in order to survive, it must be successfully passed on. And this transmission process comes with its own set of problems.

We are the only truly "cultural" animals on this planet, the only ones to create traditions. Other animals have their practices that they repeat and imitate, like the way certain dolphins use sea sponges to kick up prey from the seafloor, or the way chimpanzees crack open nuts on rocks, but we're in another league. We are the only ones to operate according to a cumulative framework, to create extended chains of shared habits, practices, and behaviors. I'm not speaking only of social behavior or group habits—the analytical approach in this case is a bit more abstract, since we're dealing with Culture, which we're here treating somewhat hamhandedly as if it were an all-in-one package. But the point is this: humans transmit this cultural package (ideas, habits, social propensities, and much more) far and wide, and more so than any other species. And when this transmission process proves successful on a large scale, a tradition is born.

By now we've learned that this mechanism doesn't operate solely on imitation. Any attempt by one individual to precisely imitate another individual's behavior is doomed to failure—inevitably that behavior will be changed. Traditions are pliant, moldable "objects": they cannot be transmitted without a certain degree of alteration. A little like the game telephone: we start passing the message around from person to person, and in just a few rounds the errors accumulate and we're left with a completely different message. So what is it that allows a tradition to stay alive? Why is it that some take root and others end up in the waste bin? What is the key to success? And why is it that certain scripts come and go overnight, and others spread like a virus (that insidious alphabet)?

FLOPS

Successful traditions, the ones with staying power, don't depend on the faithfulness with which they're transmitted. In fact, it's the other way around. Not only does accuracy not matter; there's no place for it at all, since the original messages change so much by default, as we know from telephone. What counts is the quantity and the radius of distribution. No need for it to spread in a sudden burst, like a viral tweet, everywhere one day and forgotten the next, like this year's summer jam or beach read. No, these are destined to fade, since they're not made up of "tradition" but of "episodes." Here, we're talking about something much more tangible, more durable, something we pass on from generation to generation. To make a certain phenomenon stick like flypaper to culture, your regular old methods of transmission won't suffice. It takes something more.

Olivier Morin, an anthropologist and psychologist at the Max Planck Institute in Jena, summed up the secret in three indelible words: *repetition, redundancy, proliferation.** The more a tradition is repeated, in great quantity and over a broad territory, the longer it lasts in time. And these tides of transmission must be robust, and insistent, so as to create a continuous wave effect. Think, for example, of the Catholic mass, with its memorization, repetition, proliferation of the canon—and all for centuries and centuries. The result, across Italy and beyond, is that these prayers, whether we believe in them or not, may be the only thing that many of us know by heart, along with a poem or two we studied in middle school.

And it must also have *appeal*, more so than purpose. The thing being transmitted must have attractive elements. It must give pleasure. Traditions are not like epidemics, which propagate opportunistically and without looking anyone in the face. Selection comes into play, and in this case it's not natural† but cultural. If a tradition survives, it does so because it's bound up with cognitive preferences such as attractiveness, or because it benefits from equally high levels of repetition and diffusion.

I'll give you a random example. People are drawn to the "crime novel" genre because it's linked to so many things that lie beyond explanation: love, death, mystery, secrets. Its appeal, I'd daresay, is universal. Good table manners,

---

* Morin's *How Traditions Live and Die* (2016) is a marvelous book.

† This parallel with biology has been in vogue now for a generation. Terms like *meme* (a coinage drawn from *gene*) are at this point ubiquitous (an example of successful cultural diffusion!). A meme is an element or behavior passed through imitation or replication from one individual to another—by cultural, not genetic, means. Cultural evolution viewed through the lens of biological evolution.

though they have a universal pull, can change according to region: in northern Africa (and not only) you eat with your hands, in South Asia burping is a way of letting the host know you enjoyed your food—which shows you just how widely our ideas of appropriateness and our tolerance thresholds vary.

What is it, then, that sets one script above another? What causes the road to fork between proliferation and oblivion?

I can already hear you starting to say "utility," but I'll stop you there. Utility, "having a purpose," is not always a universal ingredient for success when it comes to a cultural element. We can't simply say that the alphabet triumphed because it's useful for something, namely for writing. All scripts are useful for writing, and none, not a single one, does it better than any other. The alphabet triumphed because historical circumstances, along with its swift and agile curves, favored its survival. Not because it's more useful than, say, the classical Cypriot syllabary.

Like everything, like all of us, scripts, too, are subject to whims, idiosyncrasies, preferences, changes, innovations, cultural revolutions. And writing, more often than you'd think, has suffered the blows of this (let's call it "fate") and come to naught.

The tales of our island and city scripts, which lasted for hundreds or thousands of years, are now behind us. All the stories I've told up to this point, with a few minor exceptions, have been success stories, stories of scripts that expanded and evolved over time. Even the undeciphered scripts that we looked at are winners, in their own way, since they lasted for a relatively long time and were transmitted from generation to generation.

In five thousand years of writing, longevity, if you take a closer look, has been hard to come by. The number of failed launches is uncountable. Though not all of them are flops. Some are examples of creations that were artfully crafted but only as an end in themselves, others are systems that were intentionally closed off and encoded, and still others are branches that never took root, the so-called *scriptae interruptae*. Let's give them a look.

Solitary Inventors

Every written thing, in the end, is destined to collapse into dust, and even the hand that writes it is reduced to a skeleton. Lines and words fall from the page, they crumble, and it's from these little dust piles that little rainbow-colored beings spring out and start leaping. The vital principle of all metamorphoses and all alphabets begins its cycle over again.

—Italo Calvino, *Collection of Sand*

If you have a secret, either conceal it or reveal it.

—Arab proverb

BLUES BROTHERS

The Blues Brothers weren't the only ones on a mission from God. So, too, were a few solitary inventors, whose achievements we'll take a look at now. Only rarely are scripts born from the mind of a single person and in a single sitting—and when it happens, like it or not, we brush paths with the transcendental. The creation of any script is mythical, invariably tied to some story of divine intervention, perhaps

its own Genesis. So it was for the Egyptians and the Mesopotamians, and with the Chinese, too, we encountered
similar inspirations. It's odd, but it's precisely in those cases
where a script is invented solo that the intervention of God,
or the gods, becomes inevitable. You'd almost think that
we humans were incapable of doing it on our own.

What we'll be examining here, however, are not inventions in the truest sense, like those we explored in previous
pages, but reinventions, adaptations of preexisting systems
with varying degrees of exposure and comprehension.
They're also constructs, writing systems designed ad hoc,
and therefore artificial instruments. This gives us reason to
reflect on the underlying motivations, which vary widely
among our lone-wolf inventors. What is it that inspired
them? The desire for secrecy, to reveal a prophecy, or else
the ambition to create an inclusive tool with a clear goal in
mind? Buried enigma or universal language? We shall see.
In all of these cases, I'll say right off, the true inspiration is
not so much God as it is the plain old alphabet.

Our lone cowboys of writing, though driven by different motives, have something in common: they are all vi-
sionaries, prophets, in the spiritual sense, but in the earthly
sense, too. They are not, at least not all of them, your typical
polished academics, experts in their field, but they nonetheless demonstrate a remarkable gift for linguistics and
a very, very keen sense of intuition. A few of them are totally illiterate, and yet no less brilliant for it. And of all the
things they might have invented, it shouldn't surprise us in
the least that the challenge they took upon themselves was
writing. Invented scripts are magical, steeped in mystery,
with secrets to conceal. Invented scripts are a test of our
cognitive abilities. They're a dare, and like all dares they're

irresistibly magnetic. Though that's not to say, at least in these cases, that they're any less artificial. Invented from an armchair.

MIGRAINE

Even a headache can lead to a script's invention. I present to you the abbess Hildegard of Bingen. Born more than nine hundred years ago, she spent practically her entire life in the confines of a monastery on an isolated hill in the Rhineland. In her more than eighty years on earth, she composed music, illuminated manuscripts, essays on biology, botany, medicine, theology. Hildegard is one of the few identifiable musical composers of the medieval period. And a woman, at that. From her stone cell, known also as "the tomb," she dispensed advice, organized the lives of her fellow sisters, and, above all, she had visions. Her visions were strange, since Hildegard seemed to see the world in a radical Technicolor 3D—dissociative hallucinations, lights and auras mixed with excruciating pain. She described everything in minute detail, illustrating what she saw in almost Chagall-like visionary drawings (though with a medieval touch).

Hildegard also provided us with an interpretation for her sickness: she attributed it to a divine revelation encompassing all five senses, "a ferocious light of extreme brilliance," as she put it. In a word: God. The neurologist Oliver Sacks, however, retroactively diagnosed her with a hellish case of chronic migraines, of the sort that can drone on for more than seventy-two hours. And it may be, in this case, that science wins out over religion. Hildegard isn't the only one who's experienced these kinds of visions.

Those who've suffered them describe a phenomenon that could very well explain what Hildegard went on to create: thoughts that emerge in a cryptic wave, the decoding of a creative message, a secret. Hildegard was able to channel her hallucinations into a concrete idea. One hell of an idea. Hildegard seized that torrent of thoughts and put it to real use. At forty-two years old, she received a message telling her to write "what you see and feel." And so she invented a script with twenty-three signs, a revelatory alphabet. *Litterae ignotae*, she called it, and she used it to record a *lingua ignota*. Hildegard's alphabet is a highly intellectual, highly erudite secret code, drawn directly from Medieval Latin (fig. 26).

What practical use did it serve? We have no idea. Per-

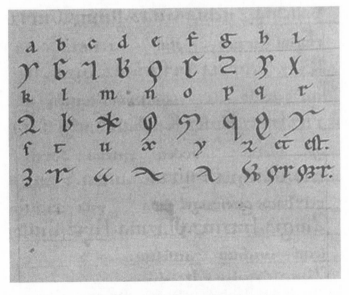

26. Hildegard of Bingen's alphabet,
the so-called *litterae ignotae*

haps she intended her *litterae* to be an unbreakable code, an enigma hidden beneath sacred letters, a guarded secret. Or perhaps Hildegard was more ambitious and wanted to create a universal communication system, steeped in God's message. A means of spreading His word around the world. We'll never know, because with all that Hildegard left us—first among which, her marvelous and deeply felt chants—she gave us no indication of the purpose behind her script. What we do know is that Hildegard could not have invented a script and a language (of which we possess only a few lines, based upon Latin grammar) in the throes of hallucination. Her design is articulate, studied, lucid. A shame, really, for something so elegant and refined to be totally useless.

THE ALCHEMIST

A two-hundred-page book, and no one's ever read it. Carbon-dated to the fifteenth century, the manuscript goes by the name of a Polish bookseller, Wilfrid Voynich, who purchased it in 1912 in Villa Mondragone, southeast of Rome, where the Jesuits kept rare manuscripts. The book is meticulously illustrated with fantastical images: chimerical plants and flowers, silhouettes of nude women, a profusion of alchemical diagrams (fig. 27).

At first glance, the images can seem to be an incoherent hodgepodge, but a more careful look reveals that the manuscript is divided into themes: botanical, the zodiac, medicine, drugs, curative baths (hence the naked women), recipes. It almost appears to be an encyclopedia of the current science, a medical manual when medicine was still tied up with alchemy, astrology, leaves, herbs, and roots. That we

27. A page from the Voynich Manuscript depicting the "bathers"

can deduce this theme at all we owe solely to the illustrations, since the writing, with its sinuous and fantastically elaborate characters, found in no other text, is illegible. A well-encrypted code, it would seem.

Human beings have always sought ways to encrypt messages: military communications, love letters, state secrets.

There are numerous ways to go about it, from the cipher developed by Julius Caesar, who employed an extremely simple substitution method, where each letter in the plain text is shifted a certain number of places down the alphabet ("a" becomes "b" and "b" becomes "c," for example), to our modern-day cryptosystems, generated by supercomputers, like the one-time pad (OTP), which are impossible to crack. So where does the Voynich Manuscript sit along this spectrum of decoding possibilities?

It's a difficult question. We know that the writing system is alphabetic, since the inventory includes just thirty signs in all. The total number of characters, however, sits around one hundred and seventy thousand, interspersed with an entire universe of graphic details (at least a million!). One hundred and seventy thousand is no small number—with modern decryption technology, deciphering the Voynich Manuscript is not quite like putting a man on Pluto. It should be possible, but so far even our modern methods have fallen short. Why is that?

Explaining the problem is simple—the trouble is finding a solution. Let's consider the characters, the whole lot of them. Let's look at how they're distributed. In any natural language, the distribution is never random: certain signs, for reasons related purely to distributive probability, appear more frequently than others (z versus a, to give just one example, is a similar case across all languages). Likewise, in any natural language, the distribution patterns are never completely formulaic; repetition cannot be a pervasive or dominant factor. In natural languages, distribution finds its sweet spot: not too many repeated formulas, not too much randomness. It's what's known as a power law. In the Voynich Manuscript this law is obeyed, the rules are respected, the distribution is similar to that of English and Latin. And yet we still have no solution.

This should give us real reason to fret: we're in all likelihood dealing with a natural language, and yet the key to unlocking its meaning remains unfathomable. Can we exclude the possibility that there's some kind of trick behind it? That the script is as artificial as the language? The Voynich is an artistic manuscript, bursting with imagination and wit. It's a valuable manuscript, illustrated with the most prized pigments, its nuanced colors still vibrant after nearly six hundred years. It's a one-of-a-kind piece, enclosed in an equally extraordinary goatskin cover. It is also, most assuredly, a work of great ingenuity—one that's been eluding and deluding us for six hundred years. For all of our technological advancement, we still haven't managed to pull back the veil. Even our recent attempt at using "machine learning" was celebrated too soon: a complete bust, in the end. All in vain.

Let's proceed by elimination. The author is not Leonardo da Vinci, or the forger-alchemist Edward Kelley, or Jacobus de Tepenec. We know from ^{14}C dating that they lived during the first half of the fifteenth century (between 1403 and 1438). A few of the architectural illustrations would lead us to believe that the book originated in northern Italy—as evinced by the swallowtail merlons on the towers, typical of that region. But we're only guessing. Whoever was behind it, they really pulled one over on us: the manuscript has still not been deciphered, and perhaps never will be. Poor Wilfrid Voynich spent his whole life trying, and he died without having made even a millimeter of progress. I can smell his frustration from here. Though at least his surname, if somewhat undeservedly, has become a piece of history.

28. A page from the *Codex Seraphinianus*

THE ASEMIC

Now take the Voynich, throw in some testosterone, a shot of steroids, and a heavy pour of Valpolicella, and you'll have yourself the *Codex Seraphinianus* (CS). In bringing it up, I'm whisking you away on a digression, since the CS has nothing to do with invented scripts. Or better yet, it has everything to do with invention—just not with scripts, per se (fig. 28).

In 1981, Luigi Serafini produced an illustrated encyclopedia of an imaginary world. In it were images of all that you might find in an encyclopedia, accompanied by scribbles meant to imitate writing—though writing they are not. My aunt Carmen, my grandmother's sister, did the same whenever she met with her spiritual guide, whom she called the wise Ibar: she'd write a random string of signs, one linked to the other, in an inspired, dreamlike *scripta continua*. Unlike my aunt Carmen, however, who was merely scribbling, Serafini was creating art, and the effect is clear and beautiful in its disorientation, and in the surreal and unexpected harmony of the world he envisions.

In the preface to the final edition of the CS (brilliantly titled *Decodex*), Serafini fills us in on the work's origins. By pairing imaginary images with equally imaginary texts, he explains, he was adopting the gaze of a small child, who looks at a book's markings without yet understanding how to read them. It's an imaginary regression to the state of wonder that comes from first encountering the mystery of writing. I, too, have memories of myself in that preliterate phase. Learning to read is one of the most magical things that a human being can achieve.

Thanks to Serafini's honesty, however, the spell of unknowing is broken. Unlike the author of the Voynich, the

author of the CS tells us openly that his writing is asemic—
that is, that it contains no hidden or encoded meaning and
is not the transcription of a language at all. It's writing, yes,
but it's hollow writing. The signs have meaning, but that
meaning is theirs alone. No point in thinking of this work
as a reflection on writing: art is not something that can be
deciphered. It simply is.

THE WIZARD

After our enchanting stroll with the CS, it's time we dive
into the tales of two men who have little to do with Hildegard's culture or the naturalistic erudition of the Voynich
Manuscript. Hildegard was overflowing with love for the
divine, and the author of the Voynich was obsessed with
detail—our next two protagonists, however, are illiterate,
unschooled, simple. But they, too, burn with a passion. And
their passion is to combat the white conqueror's abuses of
power and to reassert their own identity. We'll start with
the wizard.

Sequoyah was a silversmith born in Tennessee, right
around the time when the American colonies were de-
claring their independence from Great Britain. In these
years so crucial to the fate of the New Continent, Sequoyah
was busy fighting for a different independence, that of the
Cherokee people. He would go on to become a hero, still
celebrated to this day, though not without having suffered
along the way. Sequoyah looked on with astonishment as
he observed white men writing, and though he was illiterate he recognized the competitive advantage that this skill
gave them. They used these "talking leaves" to communicate: and this was the source of their power. It was essential

to create the same thing for the Cherokee people, to give voice to their language, to invent a writing system so that the Cherokee leaves could talk, too.

And in the process of inventing it, we'll see, it's as if Sequoyah retraced the entire course of writing's history in a single lifetime—with his first, preliterate attempts, his missteps, his persistence, molding and remolding his creation. At first Sequoyah invented a logographic system, where each sign corresponds to a word, but he soon ran into a structural problem that we're all familiar with by now: too many signs, too many abstract meanings, too many words representing "ideas." This logographic approach wasn't cutting it. So what did he do next?

During the year he spent refining his experiment, Sequoyah neglected to tend the fields, his friends mocked him, his wife threw the pages with his invention into the fire and accused him of witchcraft: to everyone else, this writing business was the work of the devil.

Sequoyah was undaunted. Ten years later he completed his work: a polished writing system that fit his language like a glove. Guess what type? A syllabary. Eighty-five signs, whose forms—though lifted from the Latin, Greek, and Hebrew alphabets, all scripts and languages he couldn't understand (he could stumble his way through English)— gave voice nonetheless, and with great precision, to the syllables of the Cherokee language. The first Native American script in northern America (fig. 29).

It would take some time before the syllabary was accepted. But Sequoyah had grit, tenacity, and above all, a plan. He taught the syllabary to his daughter, whom he then wheeled around as evidence, demonstrating just how quickly and accurately she could read a message transcribed with the syllabary. He created a "media circus" around the event and, before long, his efforts paid off. The syllabary was officially adopted by the Cherokee Nation, the percentage of literate Cherokees outgrew that of the local whites, and his success story went on to inspire some twenty other solitary inventors to create writing systems, from Alaska to Liberia.

a	e	i	o	u	v
D a	R e	T i	Ꭳ o	Ꭴ u	i v
S ga Ꭷ ka	Ꮁ ge	Ᏹ gi	A go	J gu	E gv
Ꮂ ha	Ꮅ he	Ꭿ hi	Ꮰ ho	Ꭼ hu	Ꮀ hv
W la	Ꮣ le	Ꮈ li	Ꮆ lo	M lu	Ꮈ lv
Ꮉ ma	Ꭽ me	H mi	Ꮞ mo	Ꭳ mu	
Ꮎ na Ꮏ hna G nah	Ꮑ ne	Ꮒ ni	Z no	Ꮔ nu	Ꮕ nv
Ꮖ qua	Ꮗ que	Ꮘ qui	Ꮙ quo	Ꮚ quu	Ꮛ quv
Ꮜ sa Ꭰ s	4 se	Ꮟ si	Ꮠ so	Ꮡ su	R sv
Ꮣ da W ta	Ꮥ de Ꮦ te	Ꮧ di Ꮨ ti	V do	S du	Ꮫ dv
Ꮬ dla Ꮯ tla	L tle	C tli	Ꮰ tlo	Ꮱ tlu	P tlv
G tsa	V tse	Ꮵ tsi	K tso	Ꮪ tsu	Ꮯ tsv
G wa	Ꮺ we	Ꮻ wi	Ꮼ wo	Ꮽ wu	6 wv
Ꭶ ya	B ye	Ꮿ yi	Ꭿ yo	G yu	B yv

29. The Cherokee syllabary

And that's not all. The Cherokee syllabary is still in use today, but above all it stands as a foundational ingredient in the group's linguistic, cultural, and social identity. Now they, too, have their talking leaves, and they'll never look back. Sequoyah is a national hero.

Sequoyah's story is a lesson to all of us who have ever dreamed a dream and committed our lives to making it come true. Sequoyah's story also reminds us of our obligation to understand who we are, to view our identity as a strength and not a weakness. And more still—Sequoyah's story speaks to anyone with the courage to fight against those who refuse to believe in science, who refuse to defend and nurture it every day of their lives. Sequoyah's story is a joyous exhortation to all of those who fight and, in the end, find a way to win.

THE ILLITERATE

A century or so later, on another continent, we come upon a farmer in the mountains of Vietnam, on the border of Laos, Shong Lue Yang, intent on weaving wicker baskets. Shong Lue Yang grew up knowing neither how to read nor write. He hunted squirrels and he had visions. One night, in 1959, two mysterious heavenly figures appeared in his dream and, amid an opium cloud, revealed a script. They urged him to teach it to the Hmong and Khmu peoples, so that they, too, could join the modern world and free themselves from the regime. Thus was born the Pahawh Hmong script.

Even more elaborate than the Cherokee script, Pahawh Hmong is a semi-syllabary composed of complex syllables, each in a sequence of three letters: a rime, a tone indicator, and an onset (kau, kai, kee). Normally syllables work the other way around: onset, tone, and rime. Shong Lue decided to put the rime up front, even though we still read the syllable in the standard order, with the consonant at the beginning. This inversion tells us that Shong Lue placed more importance on the rime, the syllable's vowel sound. Which is what makes this script semi-syllabic, a typology known also as an abugida, or an alphasyllabary, in which the vowels are always transcribed, but not necessarily the consonants (fig. 30).

30. An inscription in Pahawh Hmong

What's truly astounding is that Shong Lue created four progressive versions of this script, each one more linguistically advanced than the next. From revision to revision, the syllabary grew more refined, following the incredible intuition of our squirrel hunter. In the history of the world, we find no other example of such a refined innovation growing from a place of pure illiteracy. Even the least spiritual among us must admit that the human mind, with all its plasticity, is capable of miraculous things.

Shong's revelatory dream soon gave rise to a messianic movement, and Shong was heralded as a spiritual leader, with hundreds of loyal followers who learned his script and awaited his divinations. Like Lady Hao, Shong Lue Yang saw the future. Another hero who brought light and understanding to an oppressed people—a renowned figure to this day, just like the "Mother of Writing." From illiterate farmer to cultural icon, Shong Lue acquired too much power in too short a time. His wasn't a happy ending—he was murdered by the Communist regime. Of course, the textbook visionary that he was, he predicted his own assassination.

There's an important lesson to draw from these stories, which is that we should stop thinking of writing's invention as an extraordinary event. As something difficult, obscure, abstruse, rare. Examples abound of scripts created by solitary inventors, from every region of the world, revealed through dreams and visions, through the linguistic ingenuity of lone creators, or through the pure creativity of an artist.

The most recent cases—including dozens of scripts invented in western Africa, and still others in Alaska, Liberia, Cameroon, Suriname, Burma, the Philippines—are the responses of the colonized to their colonizers, who perceive writing as a status object that the latter can employ to oppress the former. In these cases (though perhaps not in all of them), writing takes on a fetishistic quality, emanating from the power held by others. To create it, to manipulate it like an object, is to seize that power.

Then there are those "revelatory" cases where writing is shown to be a divine substance, the word revealed, an ideological mission. In these interstices so charged with meaning, so material and spiritual at once, there's room as well for senseless writing, as if it were a "thing" to display in all its allusive, forbidden, untouchable power.

Writing that comes as a revelation is never revealed in full: dig and dig as long as you please, you'll still be turning up secrets.

Isolated Branches

Secrets still plague us even when we're dealing with isolated branches—scripts with no evolution, no offspring, no future.

You may not be familiar with Pokémon. Me neither. But two kids once showed me a kind of encyclopedia listing all the different Pokémon characters, divided by "race," region, and paths of development. The Pokémon world is Darwinian, with species struggling to survive, with selection and evolution. It's a complicated realm to explain, but I discovered two fundamental things: 1. There seem to be endless types of creatures, all with special powers; 2. There are certain types of creatures that never evolve, that never get stronger, more powerful, more skilled—they simply stay the same. Which, when it comes to Pokémon natural selection, is bad news.

One of these hapless victims of poké-volution goes by the name of Unown (spelling *sic*), a Pokémon belonging to the Psychic "race" (don't ask). Unown is shaped like an eye, with appendages that make it look like a letter of the Roman alphabet (think of anthropomorphized letters, but again, don't ask me why), and comes in twenty-eight forms, one for each letter (plus a question mark and an exclamation point), which are meant to resemble an ancient script (just go with it). When together as a group, it turns out, the Unown are capable of altering reality. Too bad they live rather isolated lives, trapped in their dimensions, stuck to walls like ancient inscriptions (this is the description verbatim).

As paradoxical as it may seem, the Unown Pokémon is the perfect lens through which to view our next experiments.

The time has come to speak of isolated beings, beings that never evolve, that remain barred from all development. These are systems that dawdle, that trip over themselves, and remain completely illegible as a result. We've come to the isolated branches, the most indecipherable systems of all, the childless, the truly inexplicable. The strangest scripts in the world.

We'll examine three of them, from different periods, from different regions: the New World, the Old World, and the very old world. We'll move from the most recent to the most ancient, traveling backward in time.

INCA PARADOX

The Inca are most often remembered not for what they had but for what they didn't have: the wheel, iron, a written language. This third lack has given rise to a paradox, the Inca paradox. Could it be that the largest pre-Columbian empire in the Americas existed without a jot of linguistic notation? Could someone have created the magnificence of Machu Picchu without a single sign to describe its beauty?

The answer is yes, it's possible. And if it's true that the Inca Empire is the only primary state not to have developed a writing system like the ones we've seen thus far, it's also true that it has left us something that perhaps exceeds them in technology and imagination. It's time we start thinking outside the box, looking beyond the same old flat signs. It's time we let our imaginations roam—at least for a bit.

The Inca left behind a three-dimensional system, a 3D "script." And I use quotation marks here because we shouldn't be thinking about it in conventional terms: not as simple signs engraved or inscribed or stamped on a flat surface. No. The Inca speak to us through objects. They left us a corporeal system, an extension of their fingers: long, colored cords made of the wool of alpacas or llamas. Rows and rows of cords, all strung together like charms on a necklace, all covered in knots. Picture thousands of strings, and tens of thousands of knots, a rainbow filled with messages. These are quipu (fig. 31).

31. An example of a quipu

Up until the calamitous arrival of Francisco Pizarro, quipu were used to govern an empire. For nearly two hundred years, during the fifteenth and sixteenth centuries, mathematical notations, calculations, calendars, taxes, censuses—all were tied up rationally and precisely using these Technicolor cords. And there may have been narrative works, too. Getting a firm grip on just how these quipu function linguistically, however, is no small task. There are innumerable knots that we must analyze, tied by different people, for different purposes, and spread across a vast region situated in the middle of the Andes. To get a clear sense not just of the details, but the reasoning behind them, is extremely difficult.

The most popular theory, at least up until recent times, is that quipu are mnemonic devices and nothing more, no different than the way we use rosary beads to count prayers. Quipu masters (or *quipucamayocs*) used them as a means of refreshing their memory, to keep track of the information they were recording. Or so the theory goes. Seen in this light, they would appear to be closed systems, comprehensible only to the quipu wizards who created them. But what would be the point, if it were such a hermetic device? We'd end up right back in the barren stretches of Hildegard and Voynich Manuscript territory.

Maybe there's something more behind them.

To understand how quipu function, we have to go back to being children. In school, we learn to count by using the objects around us—wood blocks, Lego, a toy abacus. We learn addition and subtraction by adding and removing objects from a pile, and by staring at our ten fingers. Then, when we learn to write and do arithmetic, we immerse ourselves in written numbers, which are abstract and two-dimensional. And this moment, though you've probably forgotten it, is the moment we lose our sense of a number's concreteness. We come to realize that 10 means "ten units of something," in a dimension with no physical objects to represent them. Abstraction takes hold of us. Without even noticing it, we all at once become platonic observers of the "idea" of number. Counting with your hands starts to feel like something primitive, infantile. Go figure.

TALKING KNOTS

The quipu system has the enthusiasm of a little kid, because it's still attached to its wood blocks, its Lego pieces. Though for all its concreteness, it's anything but primitive. The knots are used to tabulate data, following a base-ten system: the number 10, in this way, is a physical, tangible, multidimensional thing, made up of ten knots. Which makes a quipu something like an Excel spreadsheet: rows and columns and numbers, sums and totals. Not a mnemonic system, but a physical system of data representation. Not a rosary to help us rattle off mechanical litanies, but an abacus with thousands of beads, to count, to move, to manage. A physical, concrete system. Though, while Excel is fairly easy for us to read, the quipu system is, in short, another story.

Because quipu aren't limited to numbers. A third of these knotted necklaces are narrative. It's hard even to imagine that a story could be told using a series of colored knots that represent numbers, but it is so. Names, places, genealogies, songs—all are recited like so many zip codes, credit-card numbers, telephone numbers, yellow, green, and blue numbers. Because numbers, for the Inca, speak not only of quantity but of quality. I know, it's not easy to grasp, but let your imagination run free a little.

The knots are 3D, so they have form, direction, relative position, color, thickness, multiple configurations. Each element carries a different meaning: far from the body, close to the body—these distances affect what quantity is recorded. A three-dimensional Sudoku. Multivalent, multi-referential, and yet at the same time precise. According to Spanish accounts from the mid-sixteenth century, quipu were on par with the Old World's most complex scripts. One Jesuit missionary tells of an Inca woman who brought him a quipu bearing her entire life story. In knots. Incredible.

Indeed, the details of how this could have been possible are lost to us, since we don't have the legend that reveals the links among these elements (dimension, thickness, color, number, direction, etc.) and their precise meaning. We're in need of a decoder, an Inca Rosetta stone to unveil the correlations. But even without it, with this partial view of things, we can still draw a few conclusions.

BETA SOFTWARE

Have you seen the movie *Arrival*, where Amy Adams plays a linguistics professor employed by the U.S. government to translate an alien language and its enigmatic script? The aliens use a peculiar communication system, which involves squirting out circular figures like cuttlefish ink. Evanescent and ethereal, these figures quickly dissolve, leaving no trace of the message. Amy Adams studies them, and eventually comes to understand them. She deciphers their cuttlefish clouds. The film is much better than my description of it, with its muted, rainy-day tones and its almost dreamlike rhythm. There's one thing that's of interest to us, however: the aliens' signs are semasiographic.

Semasiography is a system of conventional symbols—iconic, abstract—that carry information, though not in any specific language. The bond between sign and sound is variable, loose, unbound by precise rules. It's a nonphonetic system (in the most technical, glottographic sense). Think about mathematical formulas, or music notes, or the buttons on your washing machine: these are all semasiographic systems. We understand them thanks to the conventions that regulate the way we interpret their meaning, but we can read them in any language. They are metalinguistic systems, in sum, not phonetic systems.

There are those who argue that semasiography should not be considered a form of writing in the strictest sense. If that's true, does it mean that we should be thinking of the quipu as a kind of beta software, a rough draft, prehistoric, the first phase in the development of alphabetization? Do the quipu, in other words, make the highly civilized Inca somewhat less civilized, with their roads that stretch for miles, their majestic buildings, their territorial conquests?

Absolutely not—and I don't just say that because I'm victim to the Freudian defect of overvaluing a beloved object. Strapped with governing such a vast population, taking a census of so many individuals, managing so many public affairs—because of all these necessities—the Inca decided to use an open system, one that transcended a single language, that could be most widely understood. A system that could unite them as a group.

Nevertheless, the jury's still out. And in all honesty, there simply aren't enough quipu experts to reach a definitive verdict. We scholars, too, like the Inca half a millennium before us, must come together as a group. Several digital catalogues have been created, which may one day lead to a breakthrough. Harvard's Gary Urton, with his Khipu Database (KDB), seems to have pinpointed the name of a village, Puruchuco, represented by a sequence of three numbers, like a kind of zip code. We can't rule out the possibility that this is a richly phonetic system, but we're still a long way from proving it.

To fully understand quipu, we must shed our preconceived notions of what defines writing. And stop mistaking our lack of imagination, our bias toward the "already seen," for the gaps in our knowledge of the civilization we're studying. We must keep an open mind with quipu. It may well be our limited sense of imagination that's blocking us from understanding them. Whatever the case, for all its ingenuity, the quipu system bore no offspring. It died recording its tabulations of the Inca people, giving its last few kicks in the years after the Spanish conquest.

And that's where its circle closed. Who knows if it would have had a future, if it would have become a clear, true script, had Pizarro not razed everything to the ground. I wouldn't put my money on it, but you never know.

DARKNESS

Just as promised, we're heading back to the Old Continent, to Crete, and back in time, to the age of the Aegean scripts, four thousand years ago. We must return, because hidden among these scripts is another branch, perhaps an isolate, perhaps not, but certainly the most mysterious of all. And like all the most hidden and impenetrable mysteries, it's right there before our eyes, hiding in plain sight. Along with Cretan Hieroglyphic and Linear A, which we've looked at, there's a script that's infamous among experts and wildly famous to everyone else. In Greece, it's a much abused and inflated emblem, like the Eiffel Tower in Paris or the gondola in Venice. Its image is everywhere—stamped, printed, painted, drawn, copied, prey to what is often the most gimmicky marketing and consumption—part of an idea of "Greekness" that has nothing to do with actual Greeks.

The Phaistos Disk. Phaistos is one of the great Minoan palaces, and its disk was retrieved there in the early twentieth century by an Italian archaeologist, Luigi Pernier. No archives were found in the palace—nothing like the grand archives excavated at Knossos, in the island's north, brimming with tablets of Linear A and Linear B; nor like the archives of Linear A tablets found at the Hagia Triada site, a settlement just to the south of, and contiguous with, Phaistos. At Phaistos there seemed to be no trace of writing at all. Though how could that be possible, Pernier asked himself—how could such an imposing and monumental palace, with its regal and grandiose staircases, contain only a few scattered inscriptions?

It was 1908, and the final dig was set to take place. Their funds for exploring the palace were running out. A tough moment for Pernier. Not least because, according to others around him, he was consumed with envy for his rival archaeologists and their sensational discoveries. Pernier needed his big break.

And that's exactly what he got. His discovery of the Phaistos Disk was heralded by all, rivals included, as the find of the year. Phaistos quickly gained wide notoriety. The disk astonished everyone. It was like nothing before seen (fig. 32).

How is it that such a small object—sixteen inches of humble clay—became the island's icon, the gondola of Crete? What makes it so magnetic? The answer is simple, and it's there in the crossword you do on Sunday morning, in mystery novels, in all the true-crime series on TV; in the

32. One side of the Phaistos Disk

stubborn and unrequited love that keeps you glued to your phone, waiting for a message. The answer lies in the shadows, in life's blind spots, in the rush of engaging our analytical capacities, in all our predictions and expectations of what's to come. The answer is the most alluring of all mysteries: the desire to grasp what we don't know, to get there before anyone else. To intuit, to probe. To decipher.

We're easy prey for the unknown. It binds us to the future. And the more something is shrouded in obscurity, the darker the corner, the more desperately we want to turn our flashlights on it.

Even the tiniest object, like the Phaistos Disk, is all it takes. We're hooked. A spiral of illegible, incomprehensible signs lures us into hypnosis. And the enigma lies not only in the script, but in the circumstances surrounding its discovery, its history, the doubts about its authenticity. All that revolves around the Phaistos Disk speaks of bewilderment, of trap doors and unsolved puzzles. It feels almost like a game of Clue, with a dose of Scrabble.

CHUTES AND LADDERS

What's the first thing that happens when you have a little luck, like our Luigi Pernier? The rumormongers pounce, of course. It's no more than a fraud, I tell you! A disk forged from the resentment of a bitter and envious archaeologist, desperate for glory. No chance that it's authentic. Pernier is swindling us all. The disk is a fake.

Might the rumormongers have a point? Is it really a fake? Good question. Let's case the situation: first we have an Italian (and therefore suspicious) archaeologist, caught up in a competitive environment; then we have a cash-strapped excavation campaign, down to its last drop of funding. In such a bind, one forged discovery could turn things around. And anyone who operates in the world of academia knows that it's much easier to poison the university well with wickedness and envy than it is to keep the waters clear with collaboration and dialogue.

But enough with the rumors. Let's look at the facts. What's really going on here? The disk is most certainly unusual, with its perfectly stamped symbols, its smooth and well-shaped rim. It looks like it could have been made yesterday. Even if it isn't, it sure does *seem* like a fake. And there are those who still believe it is, even among colleagues who are experts in the field. The archaeological context in which it was found, however, is solid and trustworthy. And so is its dating, attributable to the same period in which Cretan Hieroglyphic and Linear A coexisted on the island, even if in different locations. The disk was discovered near a tablet engraved in a very archaic form of Linear A. Taking all of this into account, and with the skeptics' blessing, we must conclude that Pernier never forged anything, that the disk is "good," as the slang goes. It's time we bury this fabulous tale of deceptions and hoaxes, this rumor, under all the layers of useless academic diatribes.

Enough with the tall tales. Let's pose some legitimate questions: What purpose could such a disk have served? And what's written on it?

The Phaistos Disk is not an administrative text. Its spiraling symbols recall those of another disk, from a later period, this one made of lead and inscribed in a language that to this day remains all but incomprehensible, Etruscan. Pernier cites the Magliano Disk right off the bat in his excavation report, as if to say, "full disclosure: I didn't copy anything." The two objects are very similar, though it's merely a strange coincidence. Etruria and Crete have no historical connections, and the dates are simply too far apart.

What if it's a race game, then, a kind of Chutes and Ladders? Among the thousands of interpretations, this, too, has been suggested, believe it or not. The Egyptians played a game called mehen, on circular tablets, where the track follows the shape of a coiled snake. *Mehen*, in fact, means "coiled one," the snake-god, and the track along its body marks the passage from life to death. Our modern-day Chutes and Ladders is of course less solemn, and rather less macabre. Might the Phaistos Disk be a relic of Cretan amusement, the work of some scribe bored with compiling lists of wool and sheep? I highly doubt it.

And it may be that the disk is a less isolated case than we think. Spirals were not unknown to the Minoans: we find them on rings, for example, with Linear A circling around the setting; or on your basic conical cups, the inside painted with a spiral of Linear A (fig. 33). No easy task, painting signs around the inside of such a deep goblet—and not easy to read, either. Though nothing is less legible than this disk. Its inscription—since, at the end of the day, it's an inscription that we're talking about here—is an inscrutable crossword puzzle, an impossible challenge.

Here again, we're prey to the unknown, and this time we have no choice but to concede the victory. There are certain things we must admit that we don't know, that we *can't* know, that we'll *never* know. So, shall we throw in the towel?

33. Spiral inscription in Linear A (from the inside of a cup)

BLACK SWAN

A spiraling series of symbols, on both sides, nearly all recognizable: men of various sorts and in various poses, a woman, a fish, a flower, a jar, axes, a bee, a dove, and many other figures, some of which are repeated. The Minoan world, all right there. And yet these symbols bear only a vague resemblance to Cretan hieroglyphs. Where do they come from? And what are they doing on this disk?

Nested in the mystery of this object are two other mysteries. The first is that it was baked purposefully at a high temperature to ensure its longevity. An unusual occurrence, given that the Linear A tablets and clay documents with Cretan hieroglyphs were conserved only because they were "burned," cooked in the fires that destroyed first the Minoan then the Mycenaean palaces. Baking the clay renders the tablets almost indestructible. It is therefore merely a happy coincidence that these objects were salvaged and arrived to us in near perfect condition. Let's call it the serendipity of the Aegean epigraphers.

The second mystery is that the signs are not engraved in the clay. They're stamped. The first printing—centuries before Gutenberg and his movable type, which wouldn't come until the European Renaissance of the fifteenth century. This disk is ahead of the game, with its characters all in a row, arranged in a circle. A precursor with no historical continuity, because the Cretan molds were used to stamp no other object. The Phaistos Disk is a unicum.

Two hundred and forty-two signs, in sequences of clearly and intentionally divided words, which tells us that this is in all likelihood a true written language. Though if that's the case, are we looking here at a syllabic script, like Cretan Hieroglyphic and Linear A, or a logographic script, where each sign indicates a morpheme (which is to say, a word)? The first possibility stands on better ground, but there aren't enough total signs to validate the hypothesis. And that's precisely the curse of a *unicum*. There's no way to prove or disprove anything. Not only is it an isolate, it's a black swan: rare, one of a kind, even, impossible to ignore, and cursed.

Cursed because it bars us from applying the scientific method—meaning that no one, not ever, will be able to decipher it. With subtle English irony, the philologist John Chadwick—who helped Michael Ventris decipher Linear B—wrote the following about the Phaistos Disk: "If King Minos himself were to reveal to someone in a dream the true interpretation, it would be quite impossible for him to convince anyone else that his was the one and only possible solution." Period. End of story. We're back to start in our game of Chutes and Ladders, with a dead-end track where no one wins. As they say in Rome, *alla fine del tunnel ci sono solo i fari del camion*: the only light at the end of the tunnel is the light of an oncoming truck.

BESTIARY OF THE INDUS

There are things much darker than tunnels. In the history of writing, as in life, with its distant and nebulous memories, the farther back we go in time the blurrier our perception. Yet the circumstances we find in the Indus Valley in 3000 BCE are no darker than what we encountered in Crete with its disk. You might say the two are pitted against each other in an all-out battle for who's the most indecipherable and isolated. So shrouded are they in darkness, you could distill them into Vantablack, the latest generation, which absorbs nearly 100 percent of all visible light. Pretty daunting.

We, however, operate under the conviction that if a script was codified by man, man can just as well decode it. *Humani nihil a me alienum puto*, Terence (the situation called for a flashy quote). Shall we go hunting for a glimmer of hope?

The script developed by the civilization of Harappa and Mohenjo-daro came into being very early on, almost contemporaneously with Egypt and Mesopotamia. At its height (2600–1900 BCE), the Indus Valley, which stretches from modern-day Pakistan to northern India, boasted a remarkable number of settlements, many of them small villages, though a few cities, too. It was only a hundred years ago that we discovered this magnificent culture—a sensational discovery, in that it pushed back the origins of Indian civilization by thousands of years, which up until then were dated to the rule of Ashoka, two hundred years before the birth of Christ.

Digging through the origins of this region, we can gain a sense of whether the Indo-European influence was already present, even then, five thousand years ago. If indeed it was, the implications are important to us as well, to our own origins, which are "Indo" as much as they are "European"— thousands of years old and descending from the ancient Neolithic migrations of peoples relocating to the east (India) and west (Europe).

But things are still unclear. The Indus script may indeed be hiding other, more ancient origins, buried among the Dravidian languages, and not the "Indo-Aryan" languages, which are linked to the later Sanskrit. But here we must be careful. In history's wide embrace, these linguistic attributions are often tinged with nationalistic overtones: the purity of the Aryan race, Indo-Sanskrit continuity, identity flaunted as if one could trace a direct lineage to the present.

Gaining an understanding of this script will help us to be more careful, to refrain from making brazen, biased equations, such as identity equals language, or language equals ethnicity. No such equations exist: the long path to the present day was carved by men and women on the move, by migrants, who left one home and went looking for another. Who spoke to one another and couldn't understand, who strove to communicate. And who did all of this repeatedly and in various combinations—migrating, forming new settlements, striving again and again to communicate.

Language and writing should never be linked to ideology and politics. When we decipher a script or examine a language, we do so for no greater purpose than to discover something we didn't know before. These aren't tools to be used for manipulation, to feed an ideological confirmation bias, or to throw a smoke screen over history.

But excuse me, I digress. You've now heard my plea against co-opting language for political ends. Science, and scientific data, bow to no flag.

Meanwhile, we're still stuck with a real head-scratcher. The Indus script is a mess of grand proportions—we can't even agree on a definition of what it is (talk about our inability to communicate!). We call it a script out of convenience, though the debate about its status has been raging, sometimes viciously, for years. Academics are litigious, though generally mild-mannered, creatures, and yet when it comes to the Indus Valley Script (IVS) they turn into regular gladiators. Grab your popcorn.

The majority of the "inscriptions" are found on small stone seals, only one or two inches in diameter. Nearly four thousand of them have survived—which, to those of us used to scant evidence, feels like an immense treasure. The problem is that each seal bears only a few signs, typically around five or six. And always accompanied by the figures of perfectly recognizable animals: rhinoceroses, elephants, tigers, water buffalo, zebu, and other imaginary creatures, including one that resembles a unicorn (fig. 34). Here and there we find humanlike figures in yoga poses, which may represent divinities.

34. Indus Valley Script, inscription with "unicorn"

Remember our Cretan Hieroglyphic seals? No, no connection at all with these seals from Harappa—too distant in time and place. But they can help us understand the nature of the problem. With the Cretan seals, we asked ourselves the same question, "writing, or not writing," and there, too, we dealt with signs that seem like ornaments, brief and formulaic sequences. In other words, we had our doubts, and there are those who still express resistance through gritted teeth, but we hope to have put things to rest by now. The situation here is similar, the only difference being that with the Indian seals, as you'll see, the signs are schematic, linear, and not all are icons, which means they resemble a "formal" script somewhat more than they do images. But the problem persists. And furthermore, how do we explain that Indus bestiary (minus the cobra, however)? What's it doing among such carefully traced signs? What are these animals: religious, political, genealogical symbols?

ENTROPY

Popcorn. Enter the gladiators. One team claiming it's a script, the other team, no. There's a bit of everything involved in the tussle: attempts at decipherment, algorithms, a touch of nationalism, even one or two veiled insults. Down in the arena is a mix of computer scientists, neurobiologists, archaeologists, historians, and linguists—and so begins a battle to the death.

Team NO contends that the inscriptions are not inscriptions, the signs not signs, the language not a language. The sequences are too brief, too repetitive. Too many of the signs are too rare, they appear too infrequently. Still others appear only once. "Too much" and "too little" are the mantras of nonlinguistic systems. We've already seen this applied to the Voynich Manuscript. When nonlinguistic signs enter the mix, they do one of two things: 1. They don't follow a sequential order at all; 2. They follow one too strictly, and are therefore too rigid. Natural languages are Aristotelian, they fall somewhere in the middle of these two extremes. They're flexible creatures.

Team NO, in short, believes that the IVS is indeed a system, just not a system of sounds.

So a system of what, then? The answer, I have to admit, is a bit simplistic. *Se non è zuppa è pan bagnato*, as my high school Latin teacher would say: if it isn't soup it's wet bread (an idiom not so unlike the Shakespearean "a rose by any other name").* Here, according to Team NO, are what these cursed signs represent: family and clan emblems, heraldic symbols, random religious symbols. Which would make them similar to the Neolithic symbols of the Vinča culture from southeastern Europe (around modern-day Serbia and Kosovo), or to a few of the emblems from Mesopotamia that represent gods (sun, moon, stars). Far too simple, am I right?

Far too simple. At least in the eyes of Team YES, who have thrown themselves headlong into computational computer science theory. Their game plan is to determine the probability that specific signs will follow other signs in a sequence. In "normal" languages, words or characters follow one another in an almost predictable manner. U comes after q, etc. There is, however, some flexibility to this structure—what we call conditional entropy. It's a scary name, but the underlying concept is simple. If I can grasp it, you'll have an even easier time.

Question: Can we identify statistical regularities? In other words, does the IVS bear a coherent underlying struc-

---

* Both the English *soup* and the Italian *zuppa* derive from the Gothic word *suppe*, meaning "a slice of bread immersed in broth." To call soup "wet bread," then, is to call the same thing by another name.

ture? To determine this, we look at the behavior of natural languages, like Sanskrit or Sumerian, and compare it to a sample of nonlinguistic DNA. The IVS, we find, veers closer to the languages and farther from the DNA. This alone does not prove that the system is linguistic, but it does give us a positive indication that the symbols weren't just, well, pulled out of thin air, to put it in the bluntest terms possible (no need for ten-dollar words here).

After which, Team YES—now going straight for the jugular—lands a hell of a blow: they take all of the symbols and analyze them according to their positional distribution within the inscriptions. This statistical approach, known as a Markov chain, helps determine if a sign is used more frequently at the beginning or the end of an inscription, checking for repetitions and correlations between signs that fall just before or after other signs. The Markov chain proves helpful even when the inscriptions are incomplete: once we've determined the statistical distribution, we can fill in the holes, as long as the sequences demonstrate even a small measure of repetitiveness. Not bad.

So what does Team NO have to say in response? That it's all just wishful thinking; that entropic analysis proves only that the system is neither peculiar nor rigid, which we already knew, and that "even heraldic symbols or astrological signs or Boy Scout badges have a coherent structure." Then Team YES counters, and so on, and so forth—for years! I mean it, years. And the reviews publishing these arguments aren't rags, either, or the *Podunk Paleography Gazette*, but some of the top scientific journals. Ah, those cryptographers, a difficult breed!

In the midst of all this academic squabbling, one final question remains: Was the IVS adapted from a preexisting writing system or was it invented from scratch? More likely the first hypothesis. Which bars us from counting it as the world's sixth invention, after Egyptian Hieroglyphic, cuneiform, Chinese, Mayan, and Easter Island's Rongorongo. We do have evidence of trade between the Indus Valley and Mesopotamia (especially with the Elam civilization) during the third millennium BCE. We've even found seals inscribed with the IVS in Mesopotamia and the Persian Gulf. This alone does not prove a direct transmission, but it certainly puts a bug in our ear.

Whatever happened to the IVS, after the height of the Harappa period, is anybody's guess. And we know even less about the fate of the Harappa Mohenjo-Daro civilization. This may well be the writing system that's attracted the most attempts at decipherment, and just as many failures. No mere isolated branch—the IVS was hacked clean off the tree. And with this rather autumnal image, we'll end our bout of forced isolation and head out for a little fresh air— with company.

Social Inventors

REACHING AN AGREEMENT

The experiments we've looked at thus far have brought one critical point into focus: inventing (or reinventing) is relatively easy. It's standing the test of time that's difficult. For something to stick around, as we've seen, it must be repeated, spread, proliferated. And to do so successfully requires a certain harmony of intentions.

This harmony can arise only from a group committed to maintaining, growing, and nurturing a cultural object such as writing: the group plays a critical role in institutionalizing its growth. There's nothing automatic about it. Which is precisely why our solitary inventors, whether intentionally or not, never saw the fruits of their invention flourish, either over a wide territory or through the centuries. The diameter of their creative circle stretched only so far.

To guarantee a writing system's success, then, it's essential that the members of a group come to an agreement—and, even more important, that they stick to that agreement.* In the meantime, as with all things that develop, endure, and

* An alternative method to this group effort does exist: the imposition of a writing system from on high. And we've seen numerous such cases, often

evolve, the script will change organically, even at its graphic essence: its signs will take on new forms over time.*

That said, reaching an agreement, as we all know, can be one of life's greatest challenges. We're always missing one another's intentions, explaining ourselves the wrong way around, flubbing the message. Human communication is a magnificent mess. So what can we do to start finding some common ground? Let's try adopting a little group spirit. Let's step into the living laboratory where codes are first created.

To understand how we communicate in social situations, we could attempt to reconstruct the birth and evolution of graphic (and therefore only written) symbols, as if these are events that we can observe "in vitro." This isn't quite the same as re-creating writing's invention on an experimental level, in a controlled environment, free of all surrounding noise and interference. As we've already seen, the past is full of holes and noise. Reconstructing the moment of invention, wherever it may have taken place, would be like trying to reconstruct footprints in the sand. Nothing tangible remains of those moments, nothing we can truly recover.

Through experiments on the creation of graphic symbols, however, we can retrace the birth and evolution of a shared code. How do we arrive at these symbols? How does the sharing process of these graphic systems function? And what happens to these symbols when they're passed repeat-

tied to political or religious factors. I'm thinking of the case of Atatürk, who, as a part of his great modernization project in Turkey, ruled in 1928 that citizens must use the Roman alphabet to record the Turkish language, replacing the previous Ottoman script, which was based on a consonantal Arabic *abjad*.

* Again, as long as graphic changes are not imposed from on high.

edly from person to person, thus simulating the effect of generations? And still more: How do they develop their graphic form, as they undergo this "ricochet" process?

These experiments are a kind of concentrate, since they contain all the layers of transmission in a short series of trials—they allow us to envision how we develop symbols and attempt to communicate them effectively. In these experiments, it's as if we're compressing the back-and-forth of a communication process that typically, in the "organic" evolution of symbols, unfolds over the course of generations. Through them, we can glimpse a concentrate of interactions between human beings exchanging messages.

We'll see that a few of the strategies are strangely (or perhaps not so strangely!) similar to the invention of writing. And to get writing standing on its own two feet, it takes a whole lot of dialogue. If you think about it, to get any exchange, any collaboration, any relationship standing on its feet, and standing sturdily, it always takes heaps of dialogue.

BRAD PITT

Where do symbols come from? Emblems, logos, graphic codes? It's a question I posed at the very beginning of this book. The experiment we'll look at here, conducted recently by cognitive psychologists, attempts to provide an answer.

The participants take seats around a table. Without speaking to one another, and therefore without using language (otherwise it'd be too easy), they must pass on a series of messages. All they have at their disposal is pen and paper. They must communicate, in writing, a complex or abstract concept, one that's difficult to "draw," like "soap opera," or "museum," or "parliament," or "Brad Pitt." The game works a bit like Pictionary. The "directors" of the experiment oversee the behavior of the "actors," monitoring the communication system that develops through repeated interactions.

Three things become immediately apparent: 1. The more the message is repeated, the more successfully it's communicated (*repetita iuvant*); 2. The symbols, at first, take on graphic and highly iconic forms, and over time grow less iconic, less detailed, ever more abstract; 3. After multiple interactions, the same signs come to be used to express the same meanings; therefore the participants' behavior *aligns*, it converges, growing ever more harmonious.

These three factors drive us toward the birth of graphic symbols, which consists of a fixed set of shared signs. And we can trace this dynamic evolution. Over the course of the two-person experiments (dyads), for example, the drawing for the concept "museum" begins with a plethora of details: the figure of a dinosaur on a platform, with visitors staring up at it. By the sixth exchange, the symbol has evolved, and all that's left of our poor T. rex is its spine (fig. 35).

This tells us that the more social interaction there is, the more times the participants repeat this exchange, the closer they align around the message's form, to the point of shedding nearly every indispensable detail. If we interfere a bit with the simulation, namely by adding a group of passive observers, and we then ask them to identify the symbols developed by the active participants, we find that the passive group is a little lost. They can't keep up with the development; they can't take part in the *sharing* of the message.

The graphic symbol for "Brad Pitt" suffers an even worse fate than our dinosaur (fig. 36). The Brad experiment

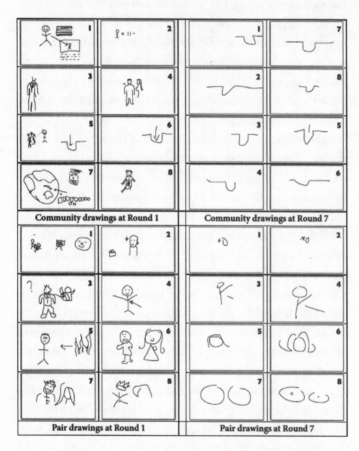

| Game 1 Participant 1 | Game 2 Participant 2 | Game 3 Participant 1 | Game 4 Participant 2 | Game 5 Participant 1 | Game 6 Participant 2 |

35. The graphic evolution of the symbol for "dinosaur"

Community drawings at Round 1 | **Community drawings at Round 7**

Pair drawings at Round 1 | **Pair drawings at Round 7**

36. The graphic evolution of the symbol for "Brad Pitt"

is not merely dyadic, or an interaction between two people, but is conducted with several people in a communication network. The group, divided into four laboratories of eight people each, simulates a mini-society: the participants exchange messages in pairs, until everyone in the group has interacted with one another, building a communication web. And what happens to Brad Pitt is even more surprising than what happens to T. rex.

Things start off just fine for Brad: many depict him with a woman, perhaps because of his quintessential good looks, perhaps to reference Angelina (the article was published before their divorce). What's surprising is that others use a rebus to identify him. Next to their portrait, they add another drawing of a pit with an arrow pointing into it, or else of an armpit, again with an arrow.

And gradually, exchange after exchange, the symbol begins to morph from its iconic and detailed origins to something more schematic and minimalist, until at last it's stripped down to the bone, just the sketch of a pit or an armpit. Poor Brad, only the "pit" of him remains.

So what do we learn from all this? We learn that even A-list actors, as "iconic" as they are at first, can be reduced to but faint images of themselves in the dynamic process of social interaction. That little by little, symbols go about simplifying themselves, once the message has been received and absorbed. That ultimately it's the interaction between human beings that determines a symbol's evolution, via the instructions we pass back and forth to one another in the chain of graphic communication. And that when we take away interaction, leaving symbols to evolve on their own in a long soliloquy, the code becomes a closed system and, rather than shed details, acquires more and more.

And finally—surprise, surprise—we learn that in establishing a convention, a shared code, we again turn to the all-powerful, universal, and instinctual rebus. This should perhaps help us to understand even more how vague a concept the "pictogram" is: language, the sound we make with our tongues, even if we shove it out the door, will always climb back in through the window. We must always give a name and a sound to things. Even when we think we're just scribbling.

ALIGNMENTS

> The better, the shorter, the easier forms are
> constantly gaining the upper hand.
> —Charles Darwin, *The Descent of Man,*
> *and Selection in Relation to Sex*

Our scribbles, from the Paleolithic to today, all move in a clear direction. While it's true that graphic systems generally shed their iconicity over time, it's not always true that they shed it completely. There are cases, like Egyptian hieroglyphs, where iconicity is maintained for centuries, even if those same hieroglyphs were also evolving in parallel toward a cursive script, known as "hieratic." So, too, with the Maya, who clung to their little faces and icons with even greater tenacity, without ever creating a parallel, more "agile" and linear form of writing.

Such devotion to the icon amounts to a strategy—a culture's means of preserving its sense of writing as an artistic, figurative, evocative object. The icon, in writing, acts as an interface with art, and this is a framework worth jealously guarding. Here we're obviously talking about forced, intentional traits, the expression of clear cultural preferences (speaking of traditions that endure!).

If we instead surrender ourselves to the natural force of evolution, we begin gradually, and inevitably, to shed iconicity. Once a code or a system is established, once it all becomes habit, the pressure on iconicity, on detail, on ornament, begins to let up. It's only when a system is "new" that details are necessary, when the code is still open-ended and the message must be recognizable.

When the system becomes closed, complete—when we've agreed upon its traits and its boundaries—we can finally relax. And this relaxation is what allowed the alphabet, for example, to so quickly drop its realistic and "pictographic" forms: the ox head, the house, water, the delta—the physical characteristics, that is, of the words being represented. Our *A*, our *B*, our *M*, our *D* all hide the legacy of these figures, a remnant of iconicity, though they've long since conformed to the conventions of the line.

We must be careful, however, to avoid the usual, simplistic interpretations of this evolution. The loss of iconicity is not linked to industrial demands, to standardization, democratization, or the need to write more, or more rapidly. It's not a question of mechanics and "intensity of use," but one of coordination, interaction, alignment.

Iconicity ceases to be necessary because the group's collective vision and the graphic system are at last aligned: the script is agreed upon, a done deal. Inessential details are no longer necessary to get the message across clearly. So long to all the trappings and trimmings—we can now afford the luxury of simplicity, without fear of botching the message or misunderstanding one another. The same thing happens with logos, which grow simpler and simpler over time, and yet remain equally recognizable. Have you noticed? And the same will happen with emojis, which will continue to grow simpler, as you'll see (though we'll speak more on this at the end of the book).

To align, when speaking of a group, means to line up, etymologically. In this case—in the life of a system of graphic symbols, that is—it indicates the almost inexorable drift toward the line. With lines we began and to lines we'll return.

SCRABBLE, CHESS, AND SCRIPTS

The experiments we've looked at reveal just how important social interaction is in the birth of graphic symbols. The greater the harmony, the simpler the system becomes. We don't even need language to get our message across successfully. All it takes is a chalkboard or a sheet of paper and something to draw with.

This isn't the only context in which language plays a marginal role. Something similar happens when scripts are transmitted from group to group. When they're adopted, readapted, reinvented.

When a group adopts a script, it doesn't necessarily mean that they all understand the language being modeled by that script. They take the model and that's all. Think back to the Cherokee we looked at earlier: Sequoyah understood very little of the alphabet, and yet he used it successfully as a "mold" or matrix for a new writing system. In this process, the script behaves a bit like a board game. Both are governed by rules that must be followed and instructions that must be explained. And, in both cases, the practice can be transmitted either by a "director," in what is known as oblique transmission (from one person to many), or in cooperation, known as vertical transmission (from person to person), though it's always a social, interactive process. Scripts and games are always part of a dynamic, group exchange of actions and reactions.

Both also undergo changes in their most fundamental elements: whether signs or rules, in time both are subject to alterations and substitutions. Games and scripts evolve, in other words, with calibrations, transformations, adjustments. They're the mice in the great laboratory of social communication.

And there's no such thing as an optimal state for either, a point of maximum perfection, at which you can say, "great, the experiment is now flawless, we'll never do any better." Like all things created by man, it's plagued by some woodworm or weakness: a redundant sign, an extra pawn, an oversight in the rules. There's a crack in everything, as Leonard Cohen said, and that's how the light gets in.

The important thing is that the language is never the protagonist. We always think of writing as a vehicle for language, an instrument, a technology. And in a certain pragmatic sense, that's precisely what writing does: it carries language on its back. Saussure, on the other hand, the father of linguistics, thought of writing as something parasitic, something subordinate to language. And he was wrong. Writing has a parallel, independent life of its own. A script can notate several languages (just think of the alphabet, which records hundreds, all very different from one another), but a language can be notated in several scripts (Greek is one example, written with the alphabet, Linear B, and the classical Cypriot syllabary). The two tracks can be interchangeable, but they always run parallel.

Writing is an object in itself. When it comes to transmission, its passage from one person to the next, language has very little wiggle room. Writing, with its signs and their forms, roams across the world and is selected, used and re-used, transported and remodeled, and, especially, adapted to other languages.

It's a similar story with board games. They're transmitted and exchanged by different groups, and they often function as a social lubricant to aid with integration. Language is not an indispensable factor. A board game can be explained merely be watching other people play. When the "foreign" observer grasps the mechanics of a game or a script, everyone involved, observers and participants alike, smiles with satisfaction, even if they can't understand one another.

Learning to recognize another's actions, mirroring, imitation, reciprocity: board games and scripts are pawns on a most human chessboard, where winning and losing count for very little. What counts, what's truly fun, is recognizing the other person's moves and gaining a firm grasp of the exchange.

BETTER TO BE IN BAD COMPANY

So wherein lies the secret to an invention's success? Not in its longevity, which is contingent upon the survival of the group that uses it. Not in solitary invention, which often dies before it even gets off the ground. The secret to success lies in a group's ability to align itself, allowing for the harmonious communication of a shared code of signs. And invention is a long, multistep process, dependent on social cooperation, group participation, the ping-pong of exchange, cohabitation, and the need to make ourselves understood.

A script's success does not lie in its simplicity, its graphic agility, its structural economy, or how easy it is to learn. Its success lies in repetition, diffusion, in the social cooperation of those who use it. In the enduring force of interaction.

Success does not lie in the spark of discovery, or in the short-lived drive toward a script's creation. This is only the beginning, which the discoverers themselves may not even be aware of. Success lies in everything that comes after: the meticulous, laborious construction of an agreed-upon set of conventions. As well as in waving goodbye to any useless, superfluous elements, details, familiarity, iconicity, to make room for the essential things, without which we cannot communicate.

Success lies in adapting, organizing, perfecting each symbol until the system is closed and clear. But the final goal is not to reach some optimal state. No such optimal state exists. Just as there's no such script that's perfectly molded to a language's every sound. In fact, because writing systems crystallize and become conventions, they always bear within themselves a number of defective or redundant elements. Such is the case with all scripts, no exceptions. In English, for example, there are several ways to produce the sound /k/ (hard "c"): *k* as in "kite," *c* as in "card," and *ch* as in "character." The reasons are historical, tied to the alphabet's passage from Greek to Etruscan to Roman (our metalinguistic board games). And yet here we are, still alive and able to understand one another all the same, defects and redundancies included. In other words, better to invent in "bad company" than alone.

Human interactions, at any rate, are always imperfect

and riddled with problems. And writing, as a product of these exchanges, is by definition an equally imperfect system. But none of these shortcomings or imprecisions spoils the broth. Nothing can stop the greatest invention in the world from relaying (however imperfectly) the most important thing in the world: our desire to be understood.

DISCOVERIES

Where to Begin

The next aspect of science is its contents, the things that have been found out. This is the yield. This is the gold. This is the excitement, the pay you get for all the disciplined thinking and hard work. The work is not done for the sake of an application. It is done for the excitement of what is found out. Perhaps most of you know this. But to those of you who do not know it, it is almost impossible for me to convey in a lecture this important aspect, this exciting part, the real reason for science. And without understanding this you miss the whole point. You cannot understand science and its relation to anything else unless you understand and appreciate the great adventure of our time. You do not live in your time unless you understand that this is a tremendous adventure and a wild and exciting thing.

These are the words of the physicist Richard Feynman, during one of the three lectures he delivered at the University of Washington in 1963.* Nearly sixty years ago.

* These three lectures make up the book *The Meaning of It All* (Addison-Wesley, 1998).

And I can't think of a single word I'd add today, to express the joy of discovery, lest I spoil the cake with a rotten cherry.

Though what I *can* do is attempt to explain what Feynman was getting at. It's a quartet of emotions, and they combine to seize both hemispheres of the brain. They are: disorientation before an abundance of possibilities (this is where you normally make a list, or at least we list-o-holics do); the bittersweet taste of doubt (next to the list we write yes, no, maybe); the shock at finding an exception to the rule, which is mostly vexing (oops, maybe the rule is wrong?). And then there's the fourth, the most beautiful: the awe we feel when we land on an elegant solution. *At last. That's it. That's the one!* This fourth emotion is rare. And when it comes, you feel like a little kid again, hopping on a bicycle for the first time.

These four things, here . . . they keep you up at night, they jolt you out of bed in the morning, with a *pyonpyon* (remember that one?). Anyone who does research is well familiar with this quartet's music, or has at least seen the score and pines to one day hear it. To experience, if only once, the fourth movement. But how do we get there?

We've made our way, at last, to the present day and the current state of scientific research. To get here, we traveled through invention, with its long shadows and obscure origins. Now it's time to examine the methods we're currently using to solve our still unsolved mysteries, or at least to shed a little more light on them. And though we'll be speaking of the present, of current scientific studies, of the rigor of modern-day methods, this tale will launch us into the future: it's time to start looking ahead and hop on that bicycle. It's time to talk about decipherment.

DONALD RUMSFELD

Speaking of trends that latch on to our culture, do you remember the weapons of mass destruction in Iraq, the ones that were never there? It was 2002 and the U.S. secretary of defense at the time, Donald Rumsfeld, addressed us with the now immortal phrase: "As we know, there are known knowns; there are things we know we know. We also know there are known unknowns; that is to say we know there are some things we do not know. But there are also unknown unknowns—the ones we don't know we don't know." He sounds a bit like the Pokémon we met earlier.

Rumsfeld was lampooned from all sides, since it's only logical that we can't know we don't know a thing we don't know. And yet the phrase has stuck—he even built an autobiography around it (*Known and Unknown: A Memoir*), and others made a documentary (*The Unknown Known*). The idea of things that we know we don't know is not a political smoke screen tactic, however. It's lifted wholesale from an analytical technique known as a "Johari window" (fig. 37).

The name Johari is a combination of Jo and Hari, the first names of its two founding psychologists, Joseph Luft and Harrington Ingham, who developed it in the 1950s. The window is a technique that people can use to understand their relationships with themselves and others. There are four quadrants. Those on the left represent the things we know about ourselves: if something is known both to us and to others, it's out in the open; if it's unknown to others, it's a façade, a mask we wear and wear knowingly. The second column, on the other hand, represents the things that we don't know about ourselves but that others see or perceive—our weak points, in other words; as well as, lastly,

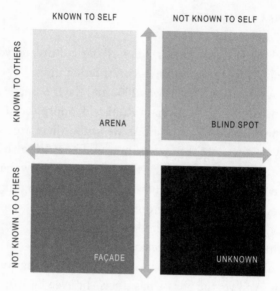

37. The Johari window

the things we don't know about ourselves and that others don't know either—the unknown unknown, terra incognita.

For the little game we're about to play, I'd like to apply this window to the relationship between the world's scripts and languages. Just as "us" and "others" are two different entities, so "language" and "writing" are two separate things. Even so, it remains a common error to mistake one for the other. But there's a stark difference between language and writing. Especially when you're talking in terms of decipherment. Because you don't decipher a language. You decipher a script. So, by replacing "us" and "others" with "languages" and "scripts" on Johari's "dashboard," we can visualize the reciprocal relationship between the two and the correlation between what's known and what's unknown (fig. 38).

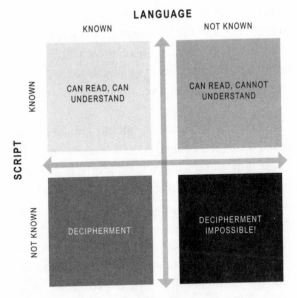

38. The Johari window reconfigured to show the relationship between language and script

In the landscape of possibilities, if we're able to both read the script and understand the language, we're in the arena of the transparent: what you're doing right now, for example, by reading these words and understanding their meaning in English, is a perfect illustration of this type of comprehension. If, however, the script is known but the language is not, all we can do is read, without understanding the language: as is the case with Etruscan. We can read it, since it's written in a modified version of the Greek alphabet, but we're not able to reconstruct its grammatical structure.

If only the script is unknown, and we suspect that the language is known, decipherment is still possible: we can apply phonetic values to the signs, and subsequently identify or confirm their linguistic basis. If, on the other hand, both the script and the language are equally unknown, it's a decipherer's nightmare, since there's little that can be done, apart from finding an analogous or sister language, where phonetic values have already been applied to the signs.

The first case—known script and known language—is in broad terms the equivalent of a translation (if the script stays the same but the language changes) or a code-switching (if the script changes but the language stays the same). For me, this is about as interesting as watching paint dry.

The second case—known script and unknown language—is more a question of linguistic reconstruction: a job for the hard-core linguists, the comparative or traditional philologists. Let them work in peace—we're talking some painstaking stuff.

The other two scenarios, however, are where *we* get to have our fun. And no small dose of it. Because the third and fourth cases are surrounded by a host of various factors, numerous crossword puzzles to be solved. Every undeciphered script has its own characteristics, its own idiosyncrasies and peculiarities, its own flaws. And the flaws are the most fun of all. Once we figure them out, we're on a beeline to that childish glee of hopping on a bike for the first time.

Like Tolstoy's unhappy families, every undeciphered script is, well, undeciphered in its own way. Which is precisely why each must be examined through a lens all its own, and accepted with all its defects. Literally, it must be taken for what it is: problematic. In the words of our old pal Donald (Rumsfeld again, not Trump): "You go to war with the army you have, not the army you might want or wish to have at a later time."

ANY OTHER STONE

> A hieroglyphic inscription's appearance is true chaos. Nothing is in its right place. There is no relation to the senses at all. The most contradictory objects are placed side-by-side, generating monstrous combinations.
>
> —Jean-François Champollion, *Précis du système hiéroglyphique des anciens Égyptiens*, 1824

The first step in battle, even before leaving, even before stepping foot off the military base, is to take clear stock of the available data. We go to war with the army we have, but we must know that army well, soldier by soldier. This means understanding which quadrant in the Johari window the script falls into, determining whether it has any kindred or similar scripts in its orbit, whether it's part of a potentially identifiable linguistic family, whether we can reconstruct its historical background and propose some basic hypotheses regarding its use. Some cases are easier to contextualize than others, but this doesn't make the decipherment any simpler. Our army is made up of human beings, and human beings are constantly making bad judgment calls.

As it turns out, the history of decipherment is riddled with blunders, errors, and, above all, prejudices. One example alone provides more than enough proof.

If I ask you for the world's most famous case of decipherment, I know exactly what your answer will be: the Rosetta Stone. And it's probably true; it probably is the most sensational decipherment. The Rosetta Stone, deciphered by Champollion in 1822, is a bilingual, trigraphic inscription—meaning that it records two languages using three different writing systems: the Egyptian language, using hieroglyphs and the demotic script, and Greek, using the alphabet.

Prior to decipherment, the reigning view was that Egyptian hieroglyphs were "sematographic," meaning that they recorded ideas, not sounds. Champollion himself agreed. But something felt off to him. You can sense as much from the epigraph earlier, taken from the *Précis*, where his frustration is almost palpable: How could this script function *ideographically*? With its strange icons and figurative symbols, how could it express a language "through a string of barely interpretable metaphors, comparisons, and enigmas"?

The script's iconicity was its own downfall. Its own hidden trap. Images couldn't possibly represent sounds. We've heard that one before, haven't we? Alas. Champollion made the logical, intuitive, simple leap: he'd already read the proper names of the pharaoh Ptolemy and of Cleopatra on the stone. It wouldn't make sense if this phonetic usage was limited to the writing of anthroponyms, it had to apply to the *entire* text: it was not some secondary usage, it was the writing system's very "soul."

You see? Years and years of prejudice and misunderstanding about iconicity meant years and years of lost time before finally reaching the goal. And this isn't the only time in decipherment's long history that we encounter this same stumbling block. Remember the delay in deciphering the Mayan script—thanks, yet again, to a misunderstanding of iconicity? And the seals with their Cretan hieroglyphs? Same problem. And the Indus Valley script? Ditto. Could it be, alas, that *we're* the ones looking at things through the wrong lens?

This gives us clear indication that in the more fortunate cases, such as Egyptian hieroglyphs, having a bilingual or trilingual text does indeed help with decipherment, but only if we don't fall prey to the power of suggestion.* We're all experts at complicating our own lives, at digging up obstacles that were never there in the first place. We love nothing more than to stick our paws in the mix and screw things up. Even when the material puts us at an advantage, we still go beating our heads against the same old preconceived notions and prefabricated ideas. We are all (not just those of us obsessed with undeciphered scripts) masters of confirmation bias. It is mankind's most formidable intellectual enemy.

And it's an enemy that strikes indiscriminately— infecting us with a desperate need for every fact and piece of data, the entire truth, to conform to an idea that we already believe in. It's an error in inductive reasoning that we fall for with alarming ease. The world must readily adapt itself to what we already think we know. It's the poor mountain that must always go to Mohammed, even when the mountain has every reason to stay put.

When this is the reality, it makes little difference

---

* There are many cases where a script has been deciphered thanks to bilingual inscriptions: for example, the classical Cypriot syllabary, deciphered in 1851 thanks to a bilingual text including a Phoenician inscription; or the Ugaritic alphabet, or Anatolian hieroglyphs. There are, on the flip side, other cases where having a bilingual text made little difference—such as the inscriptions in Etruscan and Phoenician at Pyrgi, in Santa Severa, not far from Rome, which have done little to help interpret Etruscan.

whether we have the Rosetta or any other stone, whether it's bilingual, trilingual, or quadrilingual, if we can't manage to analyze the data with neutrality and patient detachment. If, instead, we embrace the ataraxia of objectivity and approach our scripts with the impartiality and open-mindedness they deserve, we'll very quickly find ourselves passing through the first checkpoint of the scientific method.

And it's even better if we have one other thing on our side: a little luck.

SCRATCH AND WIN

Luck, as in anything else, plays no small role in decipherment. And it's even more necessary in those cases where no bilingual (or trilingual) text is available at all. However, as Pasteur said, chance favors only the prepared mind. The prepared mind, in our case, is a mind well trained in the rigor of observing phenomena. Who knows how many details pass before us—if only we took note of them . . . we might even make our own luck.

It seems that somewhere between 30 and 50 percent of all scientific discoveries are accidental. From lysergic acid diethylamide, which was originally used to treat migraines (imagine what Hildegard might have invented under the influence of LSD), to sildenafil, a onetime treatment for pulmonary hypertension now used to address a very different kind of problem faced by men in the heat of passion. The serendipity of an unexpected discovery awaits only those with the eyes and brain to seize it. To read the signs well and act in accordance. It doesn't happen to just anyone. It takes preparation, a feel for opportunity, and a healthy dose of stubborn determination.

Luck, in short, looks no one in the face—it's up to us to recognize and scrutinize it when it crosses our path. It's up to us to interpret the clues.

In the late 1940s, a scholar at Brooklyn College in New York, Alice Kober, took a passionate interest in Linear B, eventually ceding it every minute of her free time. Alice smoked like a chimney, and she was known to file the note cards with her analytical diagrams in her empty Lucky Strike cartons (she had no problem clearing the space). So thoroughly did she study the inscriptions on the tablets that, before long, she arrived at a sensational discovery. On the other side of the ocean, Michael Ventris was just as taken with Linear B, sidelining his career as an architect to dedicate himself full-time to deciphering the script (which he'd achieve a few years later).

In the meantime, Alice Kober had the lead. In every aspect: her study methods, her intuition, her ability to seize her own good luck. She understood that the language hiding behind Linear B is inflected, with endings that change according to case, gender, number, like Latin, like Spanish (*lupus, lupi, lupo, lupum*, etc., or, in Spanish, *beso* in the singular, *besos* in the plural). She recognized roots, suffixes, and all without reading a thing, without applying phonetic value to a single sign. She rejected, and rightly so, all unfounded speculation; she cut no corners.

But Linear B is a syllabary, therefore the suffixes attached to the roots follow a particular grammatical pattern (fig. 39).

39. Alice Kober's triplets, Linear B

By looking at an example in Latin we can get a clearer sense of how these suffixes function. Let's take the word *dominus* (meaning "master") and divide it into syllables, following the declension:

> do-mi-**nus**
> do-mi-**ni**
> do-mi-**no**

The final syllable begins with the same consonant ("n" in this example), but the vowels that follow change according to the case (here "u," "i," and "o," for the nominative, genitive, and dative, respectively). This must mean that if we take a different word, for example,

> po-pu-**lus**
> po-pu-**li**
> po-pu-**lo**

the final syllable's consonant will remain the same, and the vowel will again change according to the case. And here Alice gives proof of her brilliance. She recognizes that the suffix's vowel changes in vertical position, down the line of a single word's declension (because the case changes, *-nus, -ni, -no* or *-lus, -li, -lo*), but stays the same in horizontal position, from word to word in the same conjugation (*domi-ni, popu-li*), where instead it's the consonant that changes. She constructs a tentative grid, same vowel, different consonant. She outlines a pattern of correlations. She lays the foundation.

Michael Ventris was an incredibly lucky man. Without Alice's intuitions, who knows if he'd have been able to decipher the script as he did, applying phonetic value to nearly all of the signs (and we'll look at how in a moment). Alice died just before his decipherment, unfortunately. Followed by Michael himself, only two years later, at the age of thirty-four, in a car crash (there have been mentions of a possible suicide). Two stories cut far too short.

Though when it came to deciphering Linear B, both had their share of luck. And luck, in this case, meant the serendipity of having (multiple and highly regular) patterns of repetition at their disposal, which allowed Alice to construct her mute grids of declensions. With no bilingual text available, with no concrete idea about which language might be lurking behind the script (Ventris himself, some fifteen years earlier, was convinced that the culprit was Etruscan, not Greek), the system may well have proved an impenetrable little fort.

Michael Ventris, I repeat, was a very lucky man. Kober's "triplets" (let's call them little "hat tricks," why not?) provided him with a major assist in his decipherment. And Kober, in her turn, showed great intuition, by trusting in her own eye and its magnetic attraction to all repetition. *Repetita iuvant*, as they say—and sometimes they *iuvant* a great deal.

THE GOLD

We've looked at three preconditions for a potential decipherment: the script-language relationship, with its varying degrees of "unknown"; the competitive advantage of
having a text in multiple languages; and the serendipity
of having inscriptions of a certain type (repetitive, schematic, coherent). Now we'll turn to the factor that many
hold to be the most important, perhaps the sole variable that
makes the difference between the abyss of failure and the
joy of that fourth state of happiness (the bike, the child, etc.).

The quantity of texts. That's the whopper, that's the gold
that Feynman's talking about at the beginning of this chapter, because in quantity lies the entire potential of discovery.
With a large enough quantity of texts, words, signs, even a
monkey could decipher the script. Right? Well, not exactly.

Let's look at two cases on opposite ends of the spectrum, which, coincidentally, happen to be the Phaistos
Disk and the Indus Valley Script. The first has fewer than
two hundred and fifty signs in total, the second has thousands. Both remain undeciphered today, and probably will
forever. How can that be?

In the case of the disk, we've yet to find any clear correspondence with other related systems. Those who've tried
to trace it back to Cretan hieroglyphs or to Linear A have
had little to show for their efforts: mere vague similarities
don't get you very far. And we run into the same problem
with the second case, too—splendid solitude—though the
sheer quantity of texts should give us hope. Only it doesn't.

Quantity is a fundamental factor, but without quality
it won't necessarily get you to the finish line. Isn't that

the way it always is? Size counts, but it's never enough on its own. Etruscan stands as a sobering reminder to all those who believe in the macho, "big data" approach to decipherment. All those who so confidently take the bait, sure they've got it made, without ever stopping to consider the hook.

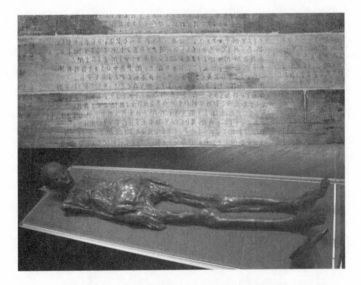

40. *Liber Linteus Zagrabiensis*, "shroud" bearing a long text in Etruscan

Take a glance at this skeleton (fig. 40), held at the Archaeological Museum in Zagreb. When discovered, it was found wrapped in a linen "shroud" bearing 281 lines in Etruscan. In those 281 lines are more than 1,300 words. A motherlode. And that's just the longest text—there are another ten thousand, of varying length. A true jackpot of signs.

And yet here we still are, wondering which family this

language belongs to, trying to reconstruct a morphology, to patch together a grammar. What is it that's causing this stalemate? The quality of the texts, unfortunately. Votive dedications, epitaphs, enchantments, names engraved on ladies' mirrors. Some of the texts are even bilingual, though it has hardly helped. The Etruscan texts are beautiful, don't get me wrong, and so, too, are the inscribed objects, extremely important for archaeologists and historians alike.

So yes, it's true that quantity holds the balance of power, we can't deny it, since it allows us to methodically confirm or refute hypotheses about how to read or identify a language. It's decisive because it helps us to reconstruct a script's skeleton and a language's paradigms. But this leaves us no less high and dry with our Etruscan skeleton in Zagreb: the problem, paradoxically, is not the amount of gold, but the cut of the metal.

TEN COMMANDMENTS

> Dear Sir or Madam . . .
> For your consideration, I enclose my proposed
> decipherment of . . .

So begin many of the emails that land in my in-box. I've already mentioned this phenomenon, and I know it's common in the field. The notes that come my way typically revolve around the Phaistos Disk and Linear A, or else Cypro-Minoan, though I've seen my share of other, more impassioned cases. Like the one on the outer-space script, brought to our planet after aliens abducted an earthling; or the one on the universal galactic language, from which all human languages descend. And that's not the only thing that's "out there" about these correspondences, as I'm sure you can imagine.

John Chadwick, whom I mentioned earlier, served as Michael Ventris's co-pilot in deciphering Linear B in the 1950s. In one of his last letters, he wrote, "I'd be obliged if those of you who come up with solutions would, kindly, *not* send them to me." Chadwick graded my written exam on Linear B in 1998, just before his death. His kindness showed through even in his most critical comments, in that very English way of being gracious and scathing in equal measure.

With much less grace, I took it upon myself to put together a list of the top ten things *not* to do when trying to decipher a script, should such a perverse idea ever cross your mind. The ten commandments of decipherment. In no particular order, though with extra emphasis on the final point, here you have them:

1. Don't mistake language for script. They are two different things, thank you very much. Linear A is not a language, nor is Linear B. Linear A's language remains unknown, Linear B's is Greek.

2. Don't fall for false similarities. Just because signs in different (even related) writing systems look similar, it does not mean they're similar in sound. This is what Sequoyah did for his Cherokee script, plucking signs at random with mixed-up phonetic values, as if from a deck of cards. Carian, an Anatolian dialect, uses letters from the Greek alphabet, though many of the sounds are changed.

3. Don't jump to conclusions. Data is neutral. Wild flights of fancy, when it comes to linguistic interpretations, are often tied to confirmation bias. Establishing a result

before you've even reached one plays no part in the scientific method.

4. It's not enough to simply "read" the signs. "Deciphering" means reconstructing the underlying linguistic structure, the grammar hidden beneath the script.

5. Follow nothing but the rigor of your methodology, your attention to happy accidents. Your intuition, too, but be judicious.

6. Don't exaggerate the possibilities. All that matters is a successful decipherment; everything else is a failed attempt.

7. Don't put forward arcane or out-of-context theories. Like the physician from Amsterdam, Becanus, who in 1580 tried to prove that Egyptian hieroglyphs were used to write Dutch.

8. Don't go looking to become a lone hero. Decipherment is no place to seek fame.

9. Don't throw yourself into impossible missions, like the Phaistos Disk. You'll end up with even emptier hands.

10. And finally, with all the brio of John Chadwick: don't get me involved.

Now that we have a sense of where to depart from, and of how we'll need to prepare ourselves mentally to face the voyage, it's time we step off the Jetway, taxi out onto the runway, and try to get this thing off the ground.

How to Decipher

> He's using a polymorphic engine to mutate the
> code. Whenever I try to gain access, it changes. It's
> like solving a Rubik's cube that's fighting back.
>
> —Q [the nerd], in *Skyfall* (2012)

The Bond villain in *Skyfall* is a cyberterrorist (an unrecognizable Javier Bardem) who uses computers to destroy the British Secret Intelligence Service, find his way to M (Judi Dench), and take her out. (Spoiler: it doesn't end well.) Some of the technology described in the film truly exists, such as the polymorphic engine in the quote above, which transforms a program into a subsequent version that still operates with the same algorithmic functionality: for example, 3 + 1 and 6 − 2 give us the same result, but they get there using a different code. So far, so good. Problem is, in the film, through the usual "Bondian" sorcery, they use polymorphic code to somehow build a map of the entire London underground.

As interesting as they are, these things have little to do with deciphering ancient writing systems. Cryptography (in the sense of "encryption") is concerned with encoding messages by converting clear information into an unintelligible form. The code is intentionally encrypted, to mask communication. Its purpose is to maintain the secret. Ancient scripts, on the other hand, have no such aim to conceal (with the exception, perhaps, of the Voynich Manuscript): if we still can't figure out how to read them, there's no one to blame but the randomness and whim of the past, the gaps in history.

The objective, however, is nearly the same in both cases. And it's called "extraction." Extraction does two things: it decodes the message and it establishes the plausibility of interpreting it. Extraction is a means of both arriving at the code and checking its validity. The decipherer, therefore, must reconstruct the relationship between sign and sound, then verify these correspondences. And then, if they're lucky, identify the language.

But extraction can't do the job on its own. Every case must be calibrated using another factor, which helps us reconstruct the script's context: this factor is known as "situation," and it comprises the participants (those who invent, use, and read the script in question), the relationships between them, their environment, the how, where, and why a script is used. The stage, in other words, upon which a script performs.

Deciphering the "situation" is no easy task. We must enter the brains of the ancients, with all their conventions and decisions. We must pretend to be actors on the same historical stage, able to follow the same cues, choreography, movements, and intentions of the original actors. We must train ourselves to understand, to mimic, and to bring their thoughts back to life. Extremely difficult, but not impossible.

But before we make it to the dress rehearsal, that moment when extraction and situation come together, there's a bit of road to travel.

FIVE EASY PIECES

The five easy pieces in the film *Five Easy Pieces*, starring (an irresistible) Jack Nicholson, are anything but easy: a fantasy and a prelude by Chopin, a suite by Bach, and a concerto and a fantasy by Mozart. The protagonist, Robert Eroica Dupea, is an ex–piano prodigy who's abandoned his aspirations and set off on another, sadder path. The film is not about music, it's about the difficulty of accepting how hard it is to accept your life. So much simpler to give in to frustration, resignation, and rage, to throw in the towel. Our five pieces of decipherment are even easier than the piano pieces in the film, but they teach us a similar lesson.

Decipherment, too, can be divided into five pieces, each representing a step in a well-defined analytical chain, kind of like IKEA furniture. If a step is missing in the "assembly" guide, or if the pieces don't fit together, no decipherment is possible. We'll use the undeciphered Script X as our fake specimen, a lab rat to test our analysis, which is technical and complex. Though not so different, in the end, from putting together a cheap Swedish bookshelf.

STEP 1. INVENTORY OF SIGNS. First we examine the inscriptions in Script X, then we gather all the signs and build an inventory, a repertoire. Let's call it an alphabet, though it could just as well be a syllabary (probable), with a series—perhaps extensive, perhaps not—of logograms (highly probable). Once we've built our repertoire, we'll know from the number alone whether it's one or the other, or yet another still. If there are more than fifty signs, Script X is without doubt a syllabary. The syllabary with the fewest signs of all is the Canadian Aboriginal script Cree (45), followed by the classical Cypriot syllabary (55). Once the number of signs gets up into the hundreds, we know we're dealing with a complex syllabary, likely accompanied by a barbaric throng of logograms.

I know what you're thinking: this first step is way too easy. A C-major scale on the piano, something any four-year-old could master in a flash. Unfortunately, that's not the case. Off the top of my head I can think of three undeciphered scripts that are still stuck on this first step: Easter Island's Rongorongo, Cretan Hieroglyphic, and Cypro-Minoan. The nature of the problem varies in each case. In Rongorongo, many signs are extremely similar: Do they indicate different sounds or are they merely graphic variations? It's the age-old problem of allographs—signs that vary only minimally in how they're written. If I'm writing the letter R, I can alter it a little and make it an *ℛ*, though it still records the same sound, /r/. Our eyes are well trained, but if you fall out of the habit it can become difficult to spot the difference. With Cretan hieroglyphs, there's another problem: icons. At what point does an icon cease to be "art" and become "sign"? "Almost immediately" is the short answer, though there's no consensus.

STEP 2: POSITIONAL FREQUENCY OF SIGNS. The second step comes off as difficult, though it might be easier than the first. Once we've established the inventory, we must determine how the signs are distributed within the sequences ("words"). To do so, we must first determine if the words are separate from one another. For example, in the Old Persian of Persepolis that led to the decipherment of cuneiform, the words were clearly divided by a vertical wedge. Same for Cypro-Minoan and Linear A, where a vertical line was used to indicate separation. But this isn't always the case: archaic Greek inscriptions, along with those in Latin, use a continuous script.

There's also one important mini-step when dealing with positional frequency: in an open syllabic system (the most frequent typology, with a consonant + vowel pattern, abbreviated as CV), if a sign is always in the initial position, it is very likely to be a single vowel. When we break the word A-VE-NUE into syllables, we always isolate the A at the front. There's no other way to write it, if it's a CV pattern.

STEP 3. GRAMMATICAL PATTERNS. The third step is the one so masterfully put into practice by Alice Kober in her study of Linear B. Alice analyzed the words and broke them down. She sought out the root of each word. She studied how their suffixes or endings behaved. She looked for repetitions, testing for consistent patterns. She disassembled and reassembled, mapping out the language's internal structure. She performed a surgical dissection.

Our INSCRIBE group is busy applying a similar analysis to Cypro-Minoan. And I'll say it with full transparency: we're ravenously copying Alice's logical approach, step for step. We're having less luck, since our repetition patterns are less frequent and less clear. We have fewer data (in this case, quantity would most certainly up our quality), though despite this lack we've managed to pinpoint a substantial number of proper names in the inscriptions. In other words, we know the Cypriots Tom, Dick, and Harry, and we have an idea about what they did with their lives.

STEP 4. TYPOLOGICAL CONCATENATIONS ("NETWORK ANALYSIS"). The fourth step revolves entirely around the archaeological context. If several inscriptions in Script X are found in a certain context (for example, a sanctuary, meaning they're of a religious or votive nature) and record sequences that are also found in other contexts, or are found on objects of a different typology (for example, objects related to administration), we can trace a logical connection between the two and, if we're lucky, determine the nature of the texts. Are there names of people? Of places? Are there repeated logograms? Are there numerals used to specify quantities?

In this step, archaeology is wedded to epigraphy and the study of inscriptions. This allows us to view these texts in the macro-context of their usage, to understand what purpose they might have once served. It's like playing arpeggios on the violin. Harmonies arise naturally from the concatenation of sounds.

STEP 5. COMMON FACTORS WITH OTHER RELATED SCRIPTS. Our final step, speaking broadly at least. This one can't always be put to good use, since, as we've seen, not all scripts fall into a tight-knit group; a few stray dogs wander from the pack, and finding a place for them among the ranks is nearly impossible, unless you force it. If a script is isolated, all we can do is confirm that fact, and study it as such.

But the others, those that travel as a family, all decked out with similar signs, can be studied as a pack. First of all, we can determine whether there are derivations, adaptations, differences, and similarities in how the signs appear. For example, our Script X could be derived from Script Y, but with a number of additional signs. Which, on a purely theoretical level, might mean that X represents a different language from Y. Though that would remain to be proved.

Linear B derives from Linear A, and they have nearly 75 percent of their signs in common. Applying phonetic values from Linear B to the identical signs in Linear A proves only one thing to us clearly (and I mean strikingly clearly, no matter what anyone else tells you): the language behind Linear A is not Ancient Greek. To be able to read 75 percent of Linear A and still not figure out which language it records is a fate worse than Tantalus's. At least we can come away with some kind of reading, however approximate, however incomplete.

With Cypro-Minoan, thanks to one of INSCRIBE's researchers, we're now able to trace its lineage directly back to Linear A, sign by sign (which before had not been established). Today we can say with a certain level of confidence that Cypro-Minoan and Linear B are stepbrothers. Our reconstruction of this lineage has even helped us to read Cypro-Minoan, to an extent. It's helped us move closer, in other words, to the final step, the height of decipherment: assigning sounds to signs.

AND NOW FOR THE SIXTH

I warned you, our five pieces are by no means easy. And you haven't even seen the sixth, the most difficult—not so much to understand, but to execute successfully. Which, after all, makes it more my problem than yours. In piano player terms, this sixth step is Beethoven's Op. 101, Chopin's *Grande polonaise brillante*, Liszt's *Transcendental Études*. You get the gist. And this nod to music isn't just some pretentious comparison I've trotted out to make myself look more intellectual. The sixth step is indeed music, since it allows us to hear the language behind Script X. For our sixth piece, we attempt to apply phonetic values.

I mentioned Michael Ventris a few pages back. Alice

Kober had made it through the first five steps, but she never conquered the last. Unfortunately, she stopped right at the most glorious moment, without ever seeing the fruit of her splendid labor. Though who knows what suspicions or inklings she may have had, tucked carefully away beneath her objective lab coat. Perhaps her intuition was prodding her all along:* "Come on, Alice, it *has* to be Greek." We'll never know.

What we do know is that Ventris picked up Alice's baton and made a dash for the finish line. With Kober's syllable grids, he could see which signs shared the same consonants and which the same vowels. I don't mean to imply that from there the decipherment was a walk in the park, quite the opposite: Ventris constructed a series of experimental grids, with hypotheses and tests for potential phonetic values. And I should remind you that up to this point Ventris was still convinced that the language behind Linear B was Etruscan—meaning that he (even he!) had broken the third commandment.

But the scientific method never lies. Organizing the vowels wasn't hard: we've already seen that, in an open syllabic system (which Linear B was already known to be), a vowel in the initial position is isolated. Finding a spot for the *a* was relatively basic: it's the most frequent. Ventris gave it a shot. And fortune kissed him smack on the forehead, since his CV hypotheses included the syllables *na*, *ni*, *so*, etc. (all still in a hypothetical phase). Ventris studied the repetitions among the Cretan tablets in the palace of Knossos and found a few of these syllables grouped together: a

---

* The fifth commandment of decipherment: follow your intuition, but don't give it too much credence.

sequence with *a-?-ni-?* Amnisos was the port of Knossos, noted as Amnisos even in classical Greek texts. Perhaps the sequence was *a-mi-ni-so?* And this sequence was often found together with the word *?-no-so.*

Wait up. Moment of suspense.

Do you see it now, too?

Ko-no-so. Knossos. Bingo.

I like to imagine the expression on Ventris's face when he recognized the names of two Cretan cities, and then realized that *ko-no-so* also appeared as a feminine adjective, *ko-no-si-ja*, and a masculine adjective, *ko-no-si-jo.* The language was inflected—very Indo-European. The language was Greek. Five hundred years before the Greeks' arrival, but Greek nonetheless.

Ventris was able to extract the sounds of Greek almost without need of confirmation from other languages or scripts.* He had an ample number of texts (nearly three thousand) and, more important, he had Alice's preparatory work, with her innumerable inflection diagrams. Kober's hat-trick "triplets," and her elegant assist, set Ventris up to score an epic goal (there's never a bad time for a soccer metaphor).

Though we're not in such a bad position ourselves, with Cypro-Minoan. To prop ourselves up, we're leaning on one particular category that's (relatively) simple to identify: proper nouns. Just like Michael Ventris. Just like Thomas Young, who identified the names in the Rosetta Stone's cartouches even before Champollion.† Just like Georg

---

* In truth, the classical Cypriot syllabary has six signs in common with Linear B, and Ventris did use these parallels to help validate his findings.
† Thomas Young has gone somewhat unsung in the history of VIP

Grotefend with the Old Persian cuneiform script.* And so far we've managed to identify a good many. I've stretched our story out with this detour into the sensational decipherment of Linear B, but only to show just how indispensable statistical analysis and the constant testing of new hypotheses can be when you don't have the aid of related scripts. We have Linear A as a parallel, and can also turn to the later example of the classical Cypriot syllabary. Cypro-Minoan is stuck in the middle, sandwiched between these two reasonably legible scripts. Our goal is to get a better sense of what the whole burger tastes like.

We're still in the kitchen, in the prep phase. But we have all the ingredients. In fact, it's only in recent years that we've made such giant leaps in our understanding of Cypro-Minoan. We're now equipped with a definitive inventory of signs, two thirds of which we can already read, and an outline of the script's internal structure (its grammar, that is). We still haven't figured out which language is behind it, and so we're not yet able to connect the dots. But our hope of living the "decipherer's dream," of taking a ride on that blessed bicycle, is no longer so far-fetched.

EX MACHINA

> BEN KINGSLEY: The world isn't run by weapons anymore, or energy, or money. It's run by little

---

decipherers. His contribution to the decipherment of Egyptian hieroglyphs was fundamental. It's no wonder that at the University of Cambridge, where he studied, he was known as "the Phenomenon."

* Yet another unsung early decipherer. Georg Grotefend was a grammar school teacher with exceptional analytical skills.

ones and zeroes, little bits of data. It's all just
electrons.

ROBERT REDFORD: I don't care. [*He walks away*]
   —*Sneakers* (1992)

The world is run on codes and cyphers, John.
From the million-pound security system at the
bank, to the PIN machine you took exception to.
Cryptography inhabits our every waking moment.
But it's all computer generated, electronic codes,
electronic cyphering methods. This is different.
This is an ancient device. Modern code-breaking
methods won't unravel it.

   —Benedict Cumberbatch, in *Sherlock Holmes*,
     "The Blind Banker" (2010)

In the central courtyard at the CIA's headquarters in Lang-
ley, there's an S-shaped sculpture that's much more than a
work of art. On its surface, an artist (in collaboration with
a cryptography expert) engraved four encrypted messages.
Three of these have been deciphered—the fourth remains a
mystery. The sculpture is called *Kryptos*, and the challenge
of deciphering its messages has drawn a wide range of curi-
ous decoders, including the National Security Agency and
legions of computer whizzes. And yet, while many decipherers have indeed relied on their computers, others have
cracked the codes with plain old pen and paper.

Does that make the latter better than the former? Do they
get brownie points for having done it on paper? The answer
is no. Don't be deceived by the storied image of the brilliant
decipherer, the Renaissance man and expert linguist who
does everything by hand. These days, the study of writing,
and of decipherment, is vastly different.

It has become a cooperative field, with no more room for prophets. The mantra today is synergy. Not only of group action but of thought: epigraphists, archaeologists, anthropologists, geomatics engineers, historians, cognitivists, semiologists, and computer scientists. And linguists. Perhaps linguists above all. But that hardly matters. What matters is their united effort.

It may well be that my characterization here is more of a manifesto than an objective description of what the field looks like today. Academics, especially in the humanities, are often trapped in their own intellectual bubbles. But a field like the study of writing lends itself perfectly to a more global approach, to open-minded scholarship that sees beyond disciplinary borders.

For anyone working in the field of decipherment, it's true, there's no replacing the "traditional" method, blending paleography, archaeology, and linguistics. However, it would be very shortsighted of us to write off other potentially useful approaches a priori. I present to you the bugbear of all traditional philologists. I present to you *deep learning*.

We've already looked at how machine-based methods were used in the study of the Indus Valley Script (IVS) and the Voynich Manuscript, to uncertain effect. The culprit here, I'd guess, was a lazy reliance on computers and computers only, with no regard for our mantra above, synergy: as if technology could close the case on its own. Without the eye of the humanist, you don't stand a chance at decipherment.

Putting the pieces together, completing the puzzle of an undeciphered script, demands a combination of two powerful forces: the force of logic, and the force of creativity and flexibility.

And when it comes to this analytical plasticity, computers are far outmatched by man. They do, however, offer some advantages. With INSCRIBE we've set ourselves the goal of reconstructing the entire development of the writing systems over time, from Cretan Hieroglyphic to Linear A, Linear B, Cypro-Minoan, and the classical Cypriot Syllabary. These scripts resemble one another, as we've seen, but there are also differences, both on a paleographic level (that is, in how the signs are written) and on a linguistic level. Two of these systems, Linear B and classical Cypriot, have been deciphered. They are clear and legible, and they record a Greek dialect.

Our reconstruction is multifaceted. It's archaeological, meaning it examines the context, reconstructs how the script was used, explaining it on a macro level. But it's also paleographic, concerned with the shape of the signs, their development, their differences. And it's also linguistic, seeking to understand which sounds, if any, are being recorded, applying the methods of decipherment to scripts that remain mysterious. And it's also anthropological: we want to know *why* these scripts came about in the first place. No one before has attempted to view the Aegean scripts from such a broad perspective. So specialized are we, us researchers, so fixed on the details, and so complex are the scripts that we're working on, that adopting such an all-encompassing view is a challenge. Which is precisely why we need a diverse team, driven by synergy, all working together to assemble the pieces.

I began to talk about computers and then I abruptly pushed them aside. I did this because it's important to understand that the traditional method comes before all else. With deep-learning strategies, however, we are able to do something that up until a few years ago was unthinkable: we can now take control over what we choose to do manually.

In the last five to ten years, deep-learning algorithms have proved extremely effective at detecting similar patterns in different entities or realms. For example, a computer can be programmed to recognize the category "dog" from different dog breeds. It can learn facial recognition and optical character recognition. It can verify signatures. The possibilities are endless, but the crucial function here is disambiguation, understanding if and when like goes with like.

When it comes to the Aegean scripts, deep learning can help us in two fundamental ways:

- It can act as co-pilot in our complete reconstruction of the Aegean family of scripts.
- It can verify whether we're properly grouping like with like via the traditional method. Remember that age-old problem of allographs, when reconstructing an inventory of signs (step 1 in our decipherment method)? Deep learning helps keep things straight.

Very well. Now I'll add a third aim, as long as we're being ambitious. We want to find out if there are any patterns of morphological variation. A mouthful, I know, but what I mean is we need to re-create the internal grammatical structure of all the Aegean scripts, which will in turn help us to understand their linguistic affinities.

There's one little problem, of course: the dimensions, the big data, as you already know by now. Our data is small. The Aegean scripts appear in very few texts. In all, we have around ten thousand signs—and when I say "in all," I mean every single sign in every single inscription. Still, the neural-network experts in INSCRIBE have seen worse. We're working on it. We'll get there.

Our eye, though human and fallible, will never be replaced by computers. The computer is no deus ex machina, although in the cockpit there's a pilot, and there's a co-pilot. And then there's the crew. We already passed along the Jetway, a few pages back. We buckled our seat belts. Now it's time to take off.

THE GREAT
VISION

First

EVOLUTION

Let's take one quick, final leap into the past, before we turn the page and start talking about the future. Let's picture a world very different from our own—no cars, no skyscrapers, no sprawling farms, no electric light. Picture a world where conversation is the only means of communication, of building a memory of things, events, situations. Picture a world without books, without newspapers, without text messages or screens, or store signs, or street signs, license plates, billboards, labels. Picture a world *ante litteram*—or more precisely, before we offend one of my Latin professor colleagues who argues that there's more than one letter out there, a world *ante litteras*.

Not exactly an ideal situation, right?

It was most certainly a less intriguing world, before the invention of writing. Communication was possible only in real time. We had to make do with gestures, a whole choreography of hand movements, pointed fingers, furrowed brows. And we had to use our voices, our full-throated voices, simultaneously.

It's true that thinking about how the world was before an important invention does make that invention look, well, a touch too consequential. An invention does not stand as a watershed between a clearly defined before and after. Inventions don't come with the immediate awareness that, from that spectacular moment on, the fate of mankind will be forever changed. It's therefore unlikely that the people of Mesopotamia or Egypt or China had any real sense of just how valuable a thing they'd cooked up. We're not machines, we're not clairvoyants, we're not all that great at seeing the big picture. Wrapping our heads around even just the few billion years that our planet's been around is nearly impossible, and these watershed moments become so only in retrospect.

It's looking backward that allows us to connect the dots. Looking forward, on the other hand, we see only the road left to travel. Compared to the earth's 4.5 billion years, and to the two hundred thousand years that humans have been around, writing is a protozoic microbe, a newborn tadpole. Too recent to be an integral part of our DNA, too recent to factor into the genetic evolution of our cognitive mechanisms.

Writing is an object created by us and transmitted by us. It is not biological, it is not in our genes. It is, in short, a cultural gizmo. As such, no matter what form it is conveyed in, whether it be the alphabet or Chinese or Japanese characters, it must be learned. And this learning process costs us great effort, since it is an artificial, not an innate, instrument. We must learn the rules of its game.

And then, once we've mastered it, the game becomes pervasive, it besieges us. Until it becomes a regular extension of our minds. In three words, it *becomes* natural. We ourselves aren't even aware of just how important this invention is. Of how heavily the *after* weighs on us.

Though the question remains: Were we destined, as a species at its most advanced phase, after a millennia-long trial period as hominids, to arrive there naturally, to slam headfirst into the invention of writing? Was it preordained that the evolution of culture would lead, over however long a gestation period, to the day when language would become tangible and material?

The answer is no. There's nothing inevitable, deterministic, or teleological about the invention of writing.

Yes, several cultures around the world, as it's now clear, did indeed get there on their own, from separate hotbeds of invention, leaping from their own private springboards. These hotbeds suggest that there must have been something in the soil, predisposing these regions to invention. Something must have paved the way, provided an affordance, an invitation for writing to exist. Where does this invitation come from? We're now entering the minefield of necessity. We've just gotten off the ground, and already there's turbulence.

NECESSITY

> In effect natural selection operates upon the products of chance and can feed nowhere else; but it operates in a domain of very demanding conditions, and from this domain chance is barred.
>
> —Jacques Monod, *Chance and Necessity*

One day man decides to stay put. He discovers that by plowing the fields he can fulfill all his basic nutritional needs as well as produce a rich surplus for his family, his group, and for periods of famine. Man stays put and starts producing so much that he can diversify his production. Man also marks his territory: he creates institutions, the

temple, the warehouse, the archive. Man creates bureaucracy to manage his entire magnificent creation. And what
is it that he does to secure this advantage over other men,
who inevitably, thanks to his shrewd centralization strategy, have become his underlings?

He invents writing, says Jared Diamond in *Guns,
Germs, and Steel.*

And he creates an empire. Empires, as we know, produce a great number of things. Things that must be over-
seen, that must be expedited, that must be exchanged. The
human brain can only hold so much. And besides, our time
is limited, finite, one day we die. And we must keep track
of all this, along with heaps of numbers, names of kings,
births, harvests, trades, and wars, debts, laws, and taxes.

And so writing is born to fulfill this need, says Yuval
Noah Harari in *Sapiens.*

Claiming necessity as the sole cause behind something
that doesn't yet exist is problematic. It offers too finalistic
an interpretation. To invent means to find a solution to a
problem, to fill a gap, an absence—but if we fail to notice
that problem or absence?

There's no denying that writing did, over time, trans-
form itself into a necessity. Somewhere along the way it became the means to a very precise end: to function as an
instrument of celebration and control, a coveted object. It
became a system. Over time, as was only inevitable, people
came to recognize its utility, to employ it not for a single
end but for a variety of ends.

The great institutions of the past, the empires, were of
critical importance not so much in the creation process
(who knows exactly who, how, and when it was invented!)
but in the process of maintaining the invention, of rendering it permanent, durable, of passing it on, spreading it

wide. Though we'd be mistaken to look at this culminating moment—visible to us only by glancing thousands of years into the past—as a project, a scheme, the result of a conscious plan.

Almost no invention is born from the force of such a mechanistic aim.

Let's not mistake cause for effect. Writing isn't born for this or that motive, for religion, for divination, nor for bureaucracy, nor for (or as) numbers. It isn't born to do something specific. It's born to do something much more general. Writing allows us to name ourselves and the things around us, and it conserves them: but this isn't writing's aim, it's an act, a realization. It's simply what writing does.

Writing is sound made visible and tangible, and as such it interacts intimately with our sensory systems, our ears, our eyes, hands, tongue. Which in no way makes it an innate faculty—quite the contrary. It merely makes it human. Writing is bound to perception, yes, our filter on the world, but also to everything the world is made of. To things themselves: concrete things, created things, the things we see around us, and even abstract, imagined things.

Writing is connected to other human inventions that were already alive and present: art, icons, symbols, abstract signs that had yet to be named. Writing is a natural continuation of these endeavors. It's no coincidence that all the early scripts arose from a strong, iconographic foundation, already established, already well under way. From paintings, engraved seals, emblems, heraldic symbols. It's no coincidence that this boiling cauldron of artistic ingenuity was the very same pot from which we fished up the first written signs. In China, Egypt, Mesopotamia, but elsewhere, too, in Crete, the Indus Valley, Easter Island: the list goes on. It's from there that the first notions of writing arose, from there that we learned to assemble an ordered code.

To have drawn writing forth from what was already there—from art, symbols, abstraction, all of it, but also from our perception of the world, from our ears, our hands, our tongues, our eyes—may well be one of the boldest endeavors that human beings have ever undertaken.

Relying on our unparalleled curiosity to understand what's not yet understood, experimenting, trying our luck with one approach after another. Writing is the direct result of this curiosity, this intuition, this drive to press just a bit further. If we want to talk about necessity, let's talk about this necessity: our irrepressible impulse to create, without a thought for what answers we might find.

MEMORY

Time for the coup de grâce: writing is something we could also do without. We know this from the part of our brain that looks like a seahorse and that controls our long-term memory. Before the invention of writing, and even after, in cultures where orality was the only means of communication, populations put their faith in the hippocampus, and trained it well.

Memory is a moldable, selective, specific phenomenon. Our neural synapses are constantly changing and their lives are brief: proteins don't last long in the brain. Everything in the brain is in flux, especially in the hippocampus, the only area where new neurons form. And yet our memories are not ephemeral; they're made of durable matter, which resurfaces when we bring those memories up, even if they're never quite the same as they used to be.

Milman Parry was a pioneer in the study of oral theory. He was one of the first to take note of the Homeric poems' formulaic character, their repetitive patterns, their recurrent expressions (the rosy-fingered dawn, the wine-dark sea, swift-footed Achilles). In the days of Ancient Greece, narrators would build off this skeleton, throwing in their variations and improvisations. And not just in Greece. Parry traveled to Yugoslavia to listen to and record bards capable of reciting thousands of lines. One of them, Avdo Mededović, could recite more than eighty thousand lines from fifty-eight different epic poems. But not because Avdo had memorized all this word for word. What he'd learned by heart was simply a framework. On top of which he spun his variations on and departures from the theme.

Before Homer, in Greece, on Crete, and in Mycenae, our scribes would never have dreamed of recording poems and epics using the syllables of Linear B. Linear B was a tool for the palaces and their intricate economic transactions. Poetry, on the other hand, was the stuff of singers, of *aoidoi*, of musicians and dancers. It was the festive spirit of the symposia, the music's rhythm, the pounding of feet on the earth. No one needed writing to sing and dance. Too bad no trace survives of these "Mycenaean" poems. We assume their existence; we have evidence and it's plausible (some of Homer's verses are very ancient, certainly as old as the Mycenaean age).

But these weren't writings. Transcribing verses, taking up "pen and paper," wasn't seen as something necessary. Even though a perfectly viable writing form was already available, rigged and ready. It makes sense, if you think about it: Do we go writing down all the lyrics to every song we listen to? Sure, every once in a while a line or two hits home and you jot it in your diary, or post it on your

Instagram, or tattoo it on your arm. Whatever the case, you're not copying it down so you can learn it—you've already learned it, probably by heart. Your hippocampus did the work all on its own.

The power of memory is astounding. Before it, all writing, even the most enigmatic, eye-catching, intriguing script, is nothing more than an appendage, an artificial extension. Even Plato, in his day, was onto the idea. In fact, he was even stauncher in his belief—lurking in the invention of writing he saw the pernicious beginnings of a disease, one that "will implant forgetfulness in the souls of all who learn it. They will cease to make use of their memories, since, relying on what is written, they'll call things to mind not from within themselves, but from without, by means of external signs."

Words found in his *Phaedrus*. A complete condemnation. And yet Plato wasn't totally off base. Look at us with our cell phones, which have basically become extensions of our brain—we who can hardly even remember our own phone number, saving PINs and passwords in apps to keep from forgetting them. We who can no longer construct the memory palaces erected by civilizations that predate the written word.

Let's linger a while with the Greeks, who understood a thing or two about memory. In one tale, recounted by Cicero, we hear of the lyric poet Simonides of Ceos, who invents a powerful mnemonic device and employs it to identify the guests at a feast, all of whom were killed when the ceiling collapsed: Simonides digs through his visual memory to recall the position of every invitee at the table, making a mental tracking shot of where they were seated.

Thus is born the "method of loci," which we still use effectively to this day (Sherlock Holmes is one practitioner, to give you a sense). We link the things we want to remember to precise points in space. Then, to recall them, we revisit this associative path in our mind, the spatial relationship between object and location. Which allows us, like Cicero, to remember what we want to say when we're giving a speech, what we want to buy at the grocery store, what chores we have that week, what clues we've gathered to track down the murderer (in Sherlock Holmes's case). We're back to making lists again, in other words, only we're not writing them down.

This ability of memory to move nimbly through physical space has now been confirmed by modern science. The hippocampus is tied not only to our memory but to our capacity to move through space, and to imagine future experiences. The neuroscientists May-Britt and Edvard Moser (then husband and wife), along with their colleague John O'Keefe, discovered the nerve cells responsible for our spatial positioning system, our internal GPS, which helps us orient ourselves and navigate when we're on the move. Their work earned them the 2014 Nobel Prize in Physiology or Medicine.

To some degree, we're still squandering memory's great potential. We're still haunted by Plato's prophecy, already well on its way to coming true—his warning of what happens when we neglect our memories, of the danger that underlies the written word, of forgetfulness, oblivion.

Writing changed the face of the world, that's undeniable. Though as far as evolution, as far as necessity, as far as the actual mechanics of our memory, we could just as well have made do without it.

Of course I'm playing devil's advocate here, to an extent,

and these provocations remain exactly that: provocations. We all know just how thoroughly writing revolutionized, simplified, accelerated our ability to store data. But this fact does nothing to make writing a more wieldy tool, nor a more agile object, nor, least of all, a more rapidly developing phenomenon. Nor, as some might claim, does it make it the greatest invention in the world.

Afterward

LATE TO THE PARTY

"Made on Earth by Humans." Elon Musk is an odd one, and full of surprises. His Tesla Roadster, launched into orbit in 2018, with Starman the mannequin at the wheel, has now completed its first lap around the sun. With the above words printed on its circuit board. This phrase is perhaps the most charming case of the overestimation of alien intelligence ever fathomed by man. To them we grant the burden of understanding that this is writing, that it carries a message, and that the message, via an alphabet, bears meanings like "to make," "humans," and "Earth." Good luck. It reminds me a little of a story told by Umberto Eco about the semiotician Thomas Sebeok. In 1984, the Nuclear Regulatory Commission consulted Sebeok after depositing nuclear waste in the Nevada desert that would remain radioactive for the next ten thousand years. His task was to devise a means of communicating to future generations that they should steer clear of the area. Over the course of thousands of years, naturally, civilizations and empires rise and fall, whole populations die out—so how, then, do we communicate with the aliens, should they arrive? The semiotician scrambled for an answer, ruling out all verbal communication, electrical signals, olfactory messages, ideograms based on conventions that are entirely our own. Even pictograms were scrapped. The only solution was to create a story and keep it alive: to pass along a narrative of radioactivity's danger, building myths and legends around it.

It's very odd that languages are human society's only substantial, rich, efficient, and stable code. We might have created a myriad of other systems, perhaps even universal ones. And yet language is the protagonist, the queen of interaction and conversation. It's highly efficient when synchronic, in the moment, with both speakers present, in the form of a dialogue. An extremely well-oiled code.

Writing, the code of written language, not so much. It arrived far later. It was a slow and gradual seaquake, roiling for millennia in its various creative hotbeds, only to then flood the world, spilling over the continents. And not only did it take us lots of time, it also showed up late. "Late" is a relative expression, though if we look at the two hundred thousand years (or so) that humans have been speaking compared with the five thousand years that we've been writing, the time gap is substantial. Writing came late to the party, in other words, after the guests had been chatting for millennia. But why?

To answer this question, we must get a sense of how written communication works, and not only when it's connected to writing. All codes that don't record a specific language—like semasiography, which we looked at earlier; emblems; mnemonic systems—are extremely limited in how much information they can carry. The precursors of writing, the nameless icons and all their limitations, help guide us in understanding the obstacles that prevented writing from blossoming before the fourth millennium BCE.

The problem, perhaps, lies in just how immovable codes can be. Codes make for heavy armor, covering a body—i.e., language—that's much the opposite: agile, dynamic, interactive, swift. Not only was writing late to arrive, it's late to act. It moves slowly, with a broadcast delay. In a word, or rather three, it's out of sync.

OUT OF SYNC

When it comes to inventing codes of communication, humans are excellent. More than seven thousand languages are spoken throughout the world, many of them nearing extinction, but the number is still impressive. Language (whether an innate faculty or not) is universal. Written codes are not. They're infinitely rarer. They're forced to be, by their own constraints.

Language is fast. Think of it like an athlete, climbing, running, jumping, moving through time and space at a dizzying speed. Writing, meanwhile, wears a heavy shell. Not only is writing slow, but it's resistant to change, and it's even a bit reactionary. Are you picturing the tortoise and the hare now? Well, it's not quite like that. This time around, the hare is actually faster.

Synchronic communication (speaking to one another in the same place, in the same moment, face-to-face) obviously comes with different characteristics from written communication. Just being present constitutes a great advantage: if there's a misunderstanding and the message doesn't come across, you can adjust the ping-pong of words. All you have to do is interrupt the person, ask again, correct the problem: the conversation can be repaired.

Writing, being asynchronous, lacks this flexibility. Written symbols can be processed in the absence of their author. And not having the participants there renders everything more difficult. Nothing can be repaired: all that's unclear remains unclear. And not having that ping-pong, that back-and-forth of "I didn't understand that, can you explain," is a real problem. Successful communication, outside of time and space, outside of the here-and-now of a direct exchange, requires a powerful medium, a code that's precise, effective, and, above all, stable. And stability, as we know, takes time. It doesn't come easily.

This is science speaking, not me. We're designed for dialogue, not monologue. We're designed to converse. Though let's not simplify things too much. Conversation has its problems, too: it's never linear; it can be fragmentary, elliptical. There's no easy way to plan what you want to say since you never know what the other person will say before you; it must be appropriate for that particular audience, etc. And this all goes down without any real structure, mind you. Yet it works—precisely because it's flexible. Try having the same conversation using a written code: not so simple, right? Which is why conversation is easy and writing much more difficult.

MAILBOX

However. I begin with a however. Because even with how unwieldy it can be, how reactionary, how slow, writing has changed each and every one of us, from within. I'm not talking about writing as a collective, distributive, or cultural revolution—the operative system of our memory or our history, whether personal or shared. Nor as a political, ideological, or religious instrument. Nor as a distinctive secret, an individual code.

I'm talking about the change that occurs in every one of us, a change rooted in our (very human) cultural evolution. Not natural, cultural. Which after more than five thousand years has clearly managed to touch our neurons. Reading has a mind-altering effect on all of us.

Brain-imaging experiments using MRI scans have shown that learning to read reconfigures our cognitive system. Seeing written signs activates large areas of the cerebral cortex, and to an even greater effect in those who are literate. The areas involved are the right occipital lobe, responsible for visual perception, and a focal area of the occipital-temporal lobe. This area has been termed the "visual word form area" (VWFA) precisely because of its active response to written words. This is the mailbox where all the words we read end up—even those you're absorbing right now. It's active in this very moment.

Writing is still too young, it hasn't yet had time to alter our DNA. Nor did it create a cognitive system from scratch. The invention of writing did not reconfigure our brain's operating system, though a revolution took place nonetheless. Our neurons learned to repurpose certain parts of the brain and use them to process signs. The areas programmed to recognize shapes and the outlines of objects were recalibrated to distinguish the shapes of written symbols. And signs, too, over the course of history, did their own adapting, not by force of a natural process but out of pure necessity, in accordance with how our brain scans the world around us, availing itself of a limited number of segments and contours. The lines we began this all with, remember?

Which is why QR codes—those little black-and-white squares that link objects to the virtual world—make perfect sense to a smartphone while our retina finds them completely undecipherable.

AFTER THE WHEEL

Let's cut to the chase, before we start looking ahead to the future. Let's draw a few conclusions. Even with all its flaws, its delays, its ancestral slowness, did the invention of writing truly revolutionize history? Is it, truly, the world's greatest invention?

Don't ask me. My confirmation bias starts flaring up even at the thought of it. Ask the people, in any country. Ask the Swedish, for example.

At the Swedish National Museum of Science and Technology, in Stockholm, there's a large room with a hundred display cases. Held in the cases are objects representing the hundred most important inventions in history. To make the selection, the museum conducted a survey of Swedish citizens (divided into cross sections of adults and children). In the Top 100 are the usual suspects, the inventions we'd all expect: the internet, the automobile, the lightbulb—along with a few other Cinderellas, like the skateboard, makeup, the padlock. A nice hodgepodge, in other words.

The inventions, like in any good classification, are ranked in order of importance. The world's greatest, according to the adults who were surveyed, is the wheel, followed by electricity, the telephone, and the computer. For kids (between the ages of eleven and twelve) the order of "greatness" is a bit different: first comes the computer, followed by the automobile, the TV, and the cell phone.

And what about writing?

Are you ready?

Thirtieth for adults, thirty-eighth for kids. Writing sits just beneath the zipper, and well beneath—wait for it—the stove. At least it beat the vacuum cleaner.

And yet many of the inventions on this very Swedish list stand on the shoulders of the thing that's been so woefully relegated to thirtieth place: the computer, the internet, the printing press (eighteenth!), the watch, the pen. These are tools that, without writing, would hardly be of use.

Tools. But writing isn't a tool. For the Egyptians, the Maya, the Chinese, the Mesopotamians, writing was a daughter of the gods. For our solitary inventors, it was a revelation, a divine gift, enlightenment itself.

For us, it's magic. And I say that unsentimentally, with science on my side. Because what you're doing at this very moment is literally magical. And I mean "literally" literally, letter by letter. You're reading words and sentences, without even realizing how quickly you're doing it, how quickly you're "processing" what's written. And the magic here lies in your ability to enter the head of someone who's not there with you, who isn't speaking to you, who isn't responding to you. Asynchrony, yes, but what a beautiful thing, this asynchrony! It's an imperfect magic trick, since comprehension is not instantaneous—it must be pondered, interrogated, and there's a margin of error. But it's in this act of pondering, of "thinking it over," that its perfection lies. It's the silence of this dialogue that's so revolutionary.

The wheel does no such thing, nor does electricity. Nor even the internet. Writing does it. You do it.

Tomorrow

In the opening pages of this book, I asked you to look closely at the things around you. Now I want you to take a look at these letters, which we call the alphabet:

a b c d e f g h i j k l m n o p q r s t u v w x y z

Cast your gaze out the window, toward the sky, above the roofs, the mountains, the passing airplanes, the clouds, the emptiness of the stratosphere, the black hole we've finally managed to photograph. More than fifty million light-years away from us. The invention of writing is no more than a dot in the world's history. The alphabet, which these days is everywhere you look, inescapable, is an even tinier dot in our evolution. A kind of epiphenomenon, an accident along the way, a blip.

Now look at this symbol:

@

The "at" sign.

It appears for the first time in 1345, in a manuscript now held at the Vatican, where it's used to replace the letter *a* in *amen*. It's come a long way since. In Italian, *chiocci-ola*, "snail"; in Hebrew, *strudel*; in Greek, *papaki*, "duck-ling"; in Dutch, *apenstaartje*, "monkey's tail" (which I can see, to be fair); in Czech and Slovakian, *zavináč*, "rolled-up pickled herring"; in Danish, *snabel-a*, "elephant's trunk *a*." In Bosnian it's *ludo a*, meaning "crazy *a*." And the options abound in Bulgarian: *klyomba*, "badly written letter"; *may-munsko a*, "monkey *a*"; *maimunka*, "little monkey"; or *ban-itsa*, a rolled-up pastry. Shall I go on?

What does all of this suggest? That our brain is fond of the letters in the alphabet—so simple, so few, so flexible—though only up to a certain point. The point when we're gripped by the need to anchor ourselves to something fa-miliar, something that's a part of us. Images.

We *need* images. Which is why we've invented emojis. And why we'll be stuck with them for the foreseeable fu-ture. In our digital age of telecommunication, we depend on emojis for nuance, to convey the gestures and expres-sions that we use when communicating face-to-face.

Face-to-face is the right way to put it. We have a pressing, almost obsessive need to see other faces. We crave those sensory responses that help us distinguish faces and their expressions. It's a question of practicality: in a world full of faces, having the perceptive capabilities to distinguish them efficiently is an advantage. Which is why we're al-ways seeing faces where they aren't (mountains,* taillights, clouds, oil stains, pieces of toast, Munch's scream, which seems to pop up everywhere).

Our obsession with finding faces in everything is no mere coincidence. It aids us in understanding what an-

---

* Italians say the profile of Monte Soratte, Horace's Soracte, near Rome, resembles Mussolini's face.

other person will do or say. It helps us interpret, to get inside someone else's head, to predict their next move. This explains our battalion of face emojis. And then the other "pictographic" emojis, such as the apple, the heart, the bee, the rose, the balloon: they're a natural extension of this.

We have a deep need for images. A need to see things. Not just spell them out. And more and more we're turning these pictographic emojis into rebuses (remember our 🐝 🍁?), especially in English where the rebus comes more naturally.

Emojis are not and never will be a written language. They do, however, stand as a stark reminder of something that we've carried with us all these thousands of years spent using the alphabet—something that, because of evolutionary constraints, we've never properly emphasized: our cursed, blessed need of iconicity.

This explains why emojis are all the rage and stenography all but dead.

DEAD LETTER

What about a hundred years from now? Will the magic of writing still be alive?

In 1900 (122 years ago), the American civil engineer John Elfreth Watkins made a number of predictions about what the world would look like in the year 2000. The article was published in a women's magazine like the kind my grandma would read when I was a little girl, the *Ladies' Home Journal*, and it's an illuminating piece. In it, Watkins predicts our move toward a digital future (without using the term *digital*, of course, though he might as well have), speaking in particular of long-distance, mobile, and live-broadcast communications (telephones, television, and screens), which we now know to have come true.

In other areas, however, such as the alphabet, he wasn't quite so prescient: it was Watkins's belief that we'd have by now abandoned the letters *c*, *x*, and *q*, finding them unnecessary. He's right about their redundancy, but nonetheless grossly mistaken. It's not his fault, though—we all know how slowly writing crawls.*

Poor Watkins; long-term predictions are never easy. And now here we are, about to try our hand at the same game. What landmark changes will we see during the next hundred years, if we're not completely extinct by then (which is highly probable)?

Here we go. We'll be using the ocean not only for fish-farming but also to cultivate algae, which we'll employ as a renewable energy source. Artificial intelligence will outstrip us, as expected, given that we already have a name for the phenomenon: the Singularity. Genetics and biotechnology, however, will compensate, bringing about an explosion of new intelligence that will all but grant us immortality: we'll upload our consciousness to a computer and live forever. We will see, perhaps, the death of death.

Let's keep going.

The brain-computer interface will be complete. Forget about virtual reality (primitive stuff), here we're talking about neuroreality, a direct biological connection, total symbiosis. Nanobots will repair our cells from within, and even record our memories. We will be able to communicate

---

* It's not the only thing he got wrong. Watkins thought there'd be no more cars in big cities, and no more flies or mosquitoes either (though with the rise of pedestrian-only downtowns and the way insects are now dying off, Watkins was looking even farther into the future, perhaps around 2100?).

telepathically: synthetic telepathy in the form of electrical signals, of course, not words.

Words, meanwhile, will nearly all be lost, given that languages—the seven thousand languages in the world today, and all their immense vocabularies—will die out: English, Spanish, and Mandarin, along with a few mash-ups between them (see Spanglish), will likely be the only languages spoken in the world.

And . . .

Our memory capacity will increase. We'll communicate through neural augmentation and brain implants. We may even manage to teleport ourselves. These scenarios aren't plot points in a science-fiction film. They're right around the corner.

As for writing? What role will it play in all this? In a hundred years this book will no longer exist in printed form. Perhaps it won't exist at all, perhaps publishing houses won't exist, not even Farrar, Straus and Giroux. There will be no paper, no more newspapers. In a hundred years none of you will be here, and neither will I, and no one, except maybe some retro bibliophile, will be able to check to see if these prophecies came true.

Some things die hard, however, and we call these things emotions. And I'm not talking about emojis. I'm talking again about our brain and our evolution.

For 200 million years now our emotional brain has been a work in progress. Our "rational" cortex, our cognitive apparatus, came later, around 1.8 million years ago. And our linguistic-symbolic development is even more recent. Emotions are as old as the earth, the most essential part of our human existence.

They come before language. Fear, rage, desire, pain. We must communicate them, to survive, to unite, to move forward. We must preserve them, in some way, for the future. We can entrust them to voice messages, videos, audio articles, the audiobooks we're all obsessed with now. We can consign them to the voice of time. But time is a breath, ethereal, ephemeral, made of air.

Think again of the images from forty thousand years ago. The Paleolithic symbols in caves. We can still see them. They're still there. The evidence of someone's emotions, perhaps someone who wished to be remembered forever. As long as there are emotions, there will be written letters.

Living letters.

Postscriptum

Even as a young boy, Stendhal knew he was the writer he would become. His behavior might have been described as maniacal, megalomaniacal, with moments of true delirium, were it not for the work he'd accomplish "later." He knew perfectly well that he had things to say. [...] His graphomania was a way of expanding the radius of a life he felt was constricted by time's brevity—a way of leaving "traces of life" on whatever space was within reach (most moving of all, among the items now held in the Bucci Stendhal collection at Milan's Sormani Library, is the powder—or tobacco—case with its interior covered in writing). And his cryptography is a way of making those traces evident by concealing them, of harnessing their secrecy, their complexity, to render them more interesting and expansive. And both of these things—graphomania and cryptography—belong to childhood and adolescence, respectively—to the discovery of writing and to its interiorization and reinvention. Children write on everything. And adolescents are always drawn to inventing "secret" scripts.

—Leonardo Sciascia, *The Mystery of Majorana*

Already at Combray I used to fix before my mind
for its attention some image which had compelled
me to look at it, a cloud, a triangle, a church spire,
a flower, a stone, because I had the feeling that
perhaps beneath these signs there lay something of
a quite different kind which I must try to discover,
some thought which they translated after the
fashion of those hieroglyphic characters which at
first one might suppose to represent only material
objects. No doubt the process of decipherment was
difficult, but only by accomplishing it could one
arrive at whatever truth there was to read.

—Marcel Proust, *In Search of Lost Time: Time Regained*,
translated by C. K. Scott Moncrieff and Terence Kilmartin

This book, like some ancient scripts, is an experiment.
I've written it as if speaking to you, as if writing never
existed, reciting the things that I've learned, studied,
and researched over the course of half my life. I followed
the same verbal impulse that I follow when giving a lecture
to my students, patching together shreds of our discussions in class, of dinner conversations, chats with friends
and colleagues and the people I love. I've simplified a good
bit, but that's less important. I wrote with my voice. As if,
in drafting these pages, the letters, the keys, the keyboard
were a hindrance, an extra motor task that slowed things
down.

And this is how I wanted the book to feel, as if dictated
aloud. I've purposefully given it an oral form, to get a sense
of just how heavy the armor of writing can be.

The result of this experiment is that, almost without realizing it, I've tiptoed around the thing I meant to write about: I've sidelined the very subject of the book. My belief, in the end, is that I've done this in order to keep my ears tuned to something else, not simply to "writing" but to that which unites us, that which we hold in common. That which makes it possible to communicate—sometimes precisely, more often imprecisely—using written sounds. Perhaps it's true, then, that when it's not tied to our emotions, our heart, our inescapable interconnectedness, writing has no purpose at all.

What does serve a purpose, however, are acknowledgments, even though they inevitably fall short: when it comes to expressing gratitude, words can never quite get it right. And so I'll start off with a few anti-acknowledgments. All the accidents, the slip-ups, the misbegotten coincidences, missed trains and delayed flights, the various sticks in the spokes. Whatever fun I had writing this book, I owe it to them.

As for my friends, I'll say only their names, which will make for some splendid examples of writing, once printed out: durable, solid, constant, just like the support these individuals gave me. Elena Caretta, Mattia Crespi (the number of times they read these words, shared their comments, their thoughts!), Elena Dusi, Lara Bloncksteiner. And Alessia Dimitri, above all, who first dreamed up this voyage, and Camilla Cottafavi and Giovanna Salvia. My deepest gratitude.

My superhuman, indomitable INSCRIBE team: Barbara Montecchi, Miguel Valério, Roberta Ravanelli, Andrea Santamaria, Michele Corazza, Lorenzo Lastilla, Eleonora Grassucci, Livia Biggi, Riccardo Gobbo, Adriano Fragomeni, Davide Facchinelli, Aris Anagnostopoulos, Eleonora Selvi, and everyone on INSCRIBE's Scientific Board—far too many to name, though I'll mention Gerald Cadogan, John Bennet, Fabio Tamburini, Massimo Warglien, Alex de Voogt.

And then, in no particular order: Alberto Rigolio, Alessandro Schiesaro, Irene Bozzoni, Giuseppe Ciccarone, Patrizia Campolongo, Raffaele Luiselli, Francesca Romana Berno, Emanuele Miola, Fabrizio Margaroli, Eleonora Litta Modignani, Giulia Biffis, Carlo Moccia, Guido Baccinelli, Chiara Adorisio, Azzurra, Lucilla, Bruno, the Gigettes, Grayson, Lucia, and my third niece, Chiara, born just after the publication of this book in Italian. Your support over the years has been the most beautiful gift I've ever received.

I'm truly grateful to my Department of Classical Philology and Italian Studies at the University of Bologna and to the Sapienza School for Advanced Studies in Rome, where the idea for this book first took shape. Fredrik Härén and his Ideas Island project, an oasis of pure tranquility. The Congregation of the Sacred Hearts of Jesus and Mary in Rome, Father Alberto Toutin Cataldo, Father Eric, and Luana Tarsi, who couldn't have been more helpful and patient during our endless process of scanning the Rongorongo inscriptions. And to the magical air of Chamois, in the Alps, where the last pages of this book took their first breaths.

The post-postscriptum I reserve for my parents. My father, who inspired me in so many ways, with his good humor and intelligence. And my mother, who's been reading me from the moment I learned to write, lending her careful attention to every single word.

I dedicate this book to Andrea Zerbini, who's no longer with us, but who lives on in the words he so often repeated and that echo to this day, "Knowledge is the only thing we live for." From A to Z, this book is for him.

Essential Bibliography

BEHIND THE SCENES

M. A. Changizi, Q. Zhang, H. Ye, and S. Shimojo. "The Structures of Letters and Symbols Throughout Human History Are Selected to Match Those Found in Objects in Natural Scenes," *American Naturalist* 167:5 (2006): 117–39.

J. DeFrancis. *Visible Speech: The Diverse Oneness of Writing Systems.* University of Hawaii Press, 1989.

S. Dehaene. *Reading in the Brain.* Viking Penguin, 2009.

S. D. Houston (ed.). *The First Writing: Script Invention as History and Process.* Cambridge University Press, 2004.

D. H. Hubel and T. N. Wiesel. *Brain and Visual Perception: The Story of a 25-Year Collaboration.* Oxford University Press, 2004.

———. "Receptive Fields of Single Neurons in the Cat's Striate Cortex," *Journal of Physiology* 124:3 (1959): 574–91.

M. D. Hyman. "Of Glyphs and Glottography," *Language and Communication* 26 (2006): 231–49.

T. Ingold. *Lines: A Brief History.* Routledge, 2007.

G. Sampson. *Writing Systems: A Linguistic Introduction.* Stanford University Press, 1985.

W. Van Langendonck. "Iconicity," in D. Geeraerts and H. Cuyckens (eds.), *The Oxford Handbook of Cognitive Linguistics.* Oxford University Press, 2007, 394–418.

G. Von Petzinger. *The First Signs: Unlocking the Mysteries of the World's Oldest Symbols.* Atria Books, 2016.

E. O. Wilson. *The Origins of Creativity.* Liveright, 2017.

UNDECIPHERED SCRIPTS

J. Baines, J. Bennet, and S. D. Houston (eds). *The Disappearance of Writing Systems: Perspectives on Literacy and Communication*. Equinox, 2008.

F. Dederen and S. R. Fischer. "The Traditional Production of the Rapanui Tablets," in S. R. Fischer (ed.), *Easter Island Studies*. Oxbow, 1993, 182–84.

S. Ferrara. *Cypro-Minoan Inscriptions: Analysis*. Oxford University Press, 2012.

———. *Cypro-Minoan Inscriptions: Corpus*. Oxford University Press, 2013.

S. Ferrara and M. Valério. 'Contexts and Repetitions of Cypro-Minoan Inscriptions: Function and Subject-Matter of the Clay Balls," *Bulletin of the American School of Oriental Research* (2017): 71–94.

S. R. Fischer. *Rongorongo, the Easter Island Script: History, Traditions, Texts*. Clarendon Press, 1997.

L. Kelly. *The Memory Code: The Traditional Aboriginal Memory Technique That Unlocks the Secrets of Stonehenge, Easter Island and Ancient Monuments the World Over*. Allen & Unwin, 2016.

M. J. Macri. "Rongorongo of Easter Island," in Peter T. Daniels and William Bright (eds.), *The World's Writing Systems*. Oxford University Press, 1996, 183–88.

J.-P. Olivier. "Cretan Writing in the Second Millennium BC," *World Archaeology* 17:3 (1986): 377–89.

———. *Édition holistique des textes chypro-minoens*. Biblioteca di Pasiphae. Fabrizio Serra Editore, 2007.

K. Pozdniakov and I. Pozdniakov. "Rapanui Writing and the Rapanui Language: Preliminary Results of a Statistical Analysis," *Forum for Anthropology and Culture* 3 (2007): 3–36.

M. Valério. *Investigating the Signs and Sounds of Cypro-Minoan*. Unpublished PhD dissertation, University of Barcelona, 2016, diposit.ub.edu/dspace/handle/2445/99521.

INVENTED SCRIPTS

R. W. Bagley. "Anyang Writing and the Origin of the Chinese Writing System," in S. D. Houston (ed.), *The First Writing*. Cambridge University Press, 2004, 190–249.

J. Baines. *Visual and Written Culture in Ancient Egypt*. Oxford University Press, 2007.

W. G. Boltz. "The Invention of Writing in China," *Oriens Extremus* 42 (2001): 1–17.

F. Coulmas. *Writing Systems: An Introduction to Their Linguistic Analysis.* Cambridge University Press, 2003.

P. T. Daniels. "The Syllabic Origin of Writing and the Segmental Origin of the Alphabet," in P. A. Downing, S. D. Lima, and M. Noonan (eds.), *The Linguistics of Literacy.* Amsterdam: John Benjamins, 1982, 83–110.

A. De Voogt. "The Caroline Islands Script: A Linguistic Confrontation," in A. De Voogt and J. Quack (eds.), *The Idea of Writing: Writing Across Borders.* Brill, 2011.

———. "The Evolution of Writing Systems: An Introduction," in N. Gontier, A. Lock, and C. Sinha (eds.), *The Oxford Handbook of Human Symbolic Evolution* (2nd ed.). Oxford University Press, in press.

I. Gelb. *A Study of Writing.* University of Chicago Press, 1963.

L. Godart. *L'invenzione della scrittura.* Einaudi, 2006.

S. D. Houston (ed.). *The First Writing: Script Invention as History and Process.* Cambridge University Press, 2004.

I. Mattingly. "Linguistic Awareness and Orthographic Form," *Haskins Laboratories Status Report on Speech Research* 110 (1992): 129–40.

P. N. Peregrine, C. R. Ember, and M. Ember. "Universal Patterns in Cultural Evolution: An Empirical Analysis Using Guttman Scaling," *American Anthropologist* 106:1 (2002): 145–49.

K. E. Piquette and R. D. Whitehouse (eds.). *Writing as Material Practice: Substance, Surface and Medium.* Ubiquity Press, 143–74.

N. Postgate, T. Wang, and T. Wilkinson. "The Evidence for Early Writing: Utilitarian or Ceremonial?" *Antiquity* 69:264 (1995): 459–80.

A. Robinson. *Lost Languages: The Enigma of the World's Undeciphered Scripts.* McGraw-Hill, 2002.

D. Schmandt-Besserat. *Before Writing* (2 vols.). University of Texas Press, 1992.

EXPERIMENTS

G. Brokaw. *A History of the Khipu.* Cambridge University Press, 2010.

A. De Voogt. "Navigating Disciplinary Boundaries: Script, Games and the Role of Language." *Evolutionary Psychology* 43:4 (2016): 498–505.

E. D'Imperio. *The Voynich Manuscript: An Elegant Enigma.* National Security Agency/Central Security Service, 1978.

S. Farmer, R. Sproat, and M. Witzel. "The Collapse of the Indus-Script Thesis: The Myth of a Literate Harappan Civilization." *Electronic Journal of Vedic Studies* 11:2 (2004): 19–57.

N. Fay, S. Garrod, L. Roberts, and N. Swoboda. "The Interactive Evolution of Human Communication Systems." *Cognitive Science* 34:3 (2010): 351–86.

N. Fay, B. Walker, N. Swoboda, and S. Garrod. "How to Create Shared Symbols." *Cognitive Science* 42:1 (2018): 241–69.

S. Garrod, N. Fay, J. Lee, J. Oberlander, and T. MacLeod. "Foundations of Representation: Where Might Graphical Symbol Systems Come From?," *Cognitive Science* 31:6 (2007): 961–87.

S. Garrod, N. Fay, S. Rogers, B. Walker, and N. Swoboda. "Can Iterated Learning Explain the Emergence of Graphical Symbols?," *Interaction Studies* 11:1 (2010): 33–50.

L. Godart. *Il disco di Festo: L'enigma di una scrittura.* Einaudi, 1994.

O. Morin. *How Traditions Live and Die.* Oxford University Press, 2016.

A. Parpola. *Deciphering the Indus Script.* Cambridge University Press, 1994.

R. P. N. Rao. "Probabilistic Analysis of an Ancient Undeciphered Script," *IEEE Computer* 43:4 (2010): 76–80.

R. P. N. Rao et al. "Entropic Evidence for Linguistic Structure in the Indus Script," *Science* 324:5931 (2009): 1165.

O. Sacks. *Migraine.* Vintage Books, 1992.

L. Serafini. *Codex Seraphinianus.* Franco Maria Ricci, 1981.

R. Sproat. "A Statistical Comparison of Written Language and Nonlinguistic Symbol Systems," *Language* 90:2 (2014), www.linguistic society.org/sites/default/files/archived-documents/Sproat_Lg_90_2 .pdf.

———. "On Misunderstandings and Misrepresentations: A Reply to Rao et al." *Language* 91:4 (2015), www.linguisticsociety.org/sites/default /files/14e_91.4Sproat.pdf.

G. Urton. *Signs of the Inka Khipu: Binary Coding in the Andean Knotted-String Records.* University of Texas Press, 2003.

The Voynich manuscript can be downloaded in high resolution from archive.org/details/TheVoynichManuscript.

DISCOVERIES

J. Chadwick. *The Decipherment of Linear B* (2nd ed.). Cambridge University Press, 1990.

R. Feynman. *The Meaning of It All*. Basic Books, 2005.

S. D. Houston. "The Archaeology of Communication Technologies," *Annual Review of Anthropology* 33 (2004): 223–50.

A. E. Kober. "Inflection in Linear Class B: 1—Declension," *American Journal of Archaeology* 50 (1946): 268–76.

———. "The Minoan Scripts: Fact and Theory," *American Journal of Archaeology* 52 (1948): 82–103.

M. Pope. *The Story of Decipherment from Egyptian Hieroglyphs to Maya Script*. Thames & Hudson, 1999.

M. Ventris. "The Cretan Tablets," BBC Radio, July 1, 1952; report on the decipherment of Linear B. Audio available online: www.bbc.co.uk/news/magazine-22799109.

M. Ventris and J. Chadwick. "Evidence for Greek Dialect in the Mycenaean Archives," *Journal of Hellenic Studies* 73 (1953): 84–103.

THE GREAT VISION

J. Diamond. *Guns, Germs, and Steel: The Fates of Human Societies*. W. W. Norton, 1999, 1997.

T. Hafting, M. Fyhn, S. Molden, M. B. Moser, and E. I. Moser. "Microstructure of Spatial Map in the Entorhinal Cortex," *Nature* 436 (2005): 801–806.

Y. N. Harari. *Sapiens: A Brief History of Humankind*. Harper, 2014.

C. Hayes. *Cognitive Gadgets: The Cultural Evolution of Thinking*. Harvard University Press, 2018.

M. Morin, P. Kelly, and J. Winters. "Writing, Graphic Codes, and Asynchronous Communication," *Topics in Cognitive Science* (2018): 1–17.

J. O'Keefe and J. Dostrovsky. "The Hippocampus as a Spatial Map: Preliminary Evidence from Unit Activity in the Freely Moving Rat," *Brain Research* 34 (1971): 171–75.

J. Winters and O. Morin. "From Context to Code: Information Transfer Constrains the Emergence of Graphic Codes," *Cognitive Science* 43:3 (2019).

Illustration Credits

1. © Silvia Ferrara.
2. Public domain.
3. © Heraklion Archaeological Museum, Crete.
4. Figure adapted from L. Godart and J.-P. Olivier, *Recueil des inscriptions en linéaire A*, vol. 5, preliminary 41 (1985), © 1985–2019 École Francaise d'Athènes.
5. © Cyprus Museum.
6. © Cyprus Museum.
7. © Adobe Stock.
8. © The General Archives of the Society of the Sacred Heart, Rome.
9. © The British Museum.
10. Public domain.
11. Public domain.
12. © Duncan Poupard.
15. Egyptian Museum, Cairo. Public domain.
16. © The National Museum of Damascus.
17. © The Metropolitan Museum of Art.
19. © Galina Dzeniskevich.
21. © Department of Anthropology, National Museum of Natural History, Smithsonian Institution, Washington, D.C.
27. © Beinecke Rare Book and Manuscript Library, Yale University.
28. From the *Codex Seraphinianus* by Luigi Serafini, Rizzoli, 2016.
31. © Machu Picchu Museum, Casa Concha, Cusco.
32. © Heraklion Archaeological Museum, Crete.
33. Public domain.
34. © National Museum of Pakistan, Karachi.
35. Courtesy of Nicolas Fay.
36. © Interaction Studies, John Benjamins Publishing Company.
37. © Silvia Ferrara.
38. © Silvia Ferrara.
39. In A. Kober, "The Minoan Scripts: Fact and Theory," *American Journal of Archaeology* 52 (1948), p. 97, fig. 8.
40. Archaeological Museum in Zagreb © Silvia Ferrara.